The Last Closet

THE REAL LIVES OF LESBIAN AND GAY TEACHERS

Rita M. Kissen

HEINEMANN
PORTSMOUTH, NH

Heinemann
A division of Reed Elsevier Inc.
361 Hanover Street
Portsmouth, NH 03801–3912

Offices and agents throughout the world

Library of Congress Cataloging-in-Publication Data
Kissen, Rita M.
    The last closet : the real lives of lesbian and gay teachers /
  Rita M. Kissen.
        p.   cm.
      ISBN 0-435-08147-0 (alk. paper)
      1. Gay teachers—United States.   2. Lesbian teachers—United
  States.   I. Title.
  LB2844.1.G39K57   1996
      371.1'008'664—dc20   96-4128
                                                                                          CIP

Editor: Lisa A. Barnett
Production: Vicki Kasabian
Book design: Catherine Hawkes
Jacket design: Barbara Werden
Manufacturing: Elizabeth Valway

Printed in the United States of America on acid-free paper
First issued casebound 1996.
Reissued paperback 1997.

99 98 97 BC 1 2 3 4 5

The Last Closet

To my family

Contents

Foreword

THE TRUTH, THE WHOLE TRUTH, AND
NOTHING BUT THE TRUTH

I WAS RAISED IN A SOUTHERN BAPTIST, FUNDAMENTALIST home. My personal journey has taken me from the small town of Lewisville, North Carolina, to the ivy-covered halls of Harvard College, to the high school classrooms in which I taught in Rhode Island and Massachusetts, and now to a role organizing teachers and community members across the country who wish to end homophobia in our schools. It's been a sometimes confusing journey, and it came wholly without a map or instructions.

If it was confusing for me, it was worse for my mom: raised in eastern Tennessee during the Depression, the wife of an evangelist, my mom was poorly equipped to cope with her son's being an openly gay teacher and, later, a national spokesperson on gay issues. But, like my best students, she knew what to do when she was confused—she asked questions.

Once, my mom asked me why I would put my career and future at risk by coming out. Why would I, the first person in our family ever to go to college, the first to have a chance to escape from the Appalachian underclass into which I was born, possibly throw it all away? I had to tell her the truth: "Because you taught me to be like this, Mom."

At first she was taken aback—I can imagine she thought that I was saying it was her fault after all, that she had made her son gay, just like fifties psychologists said strong moms would. I quickly realized I had to follow up on the comment.

"You see, Mom, you took me to church every Sunday morning, every Sunday night, and every Wednesday night of my childhood, where I was constantly taught 'Thou shall not lie.' And you, Mom, were especially strong on that point. You always said, 'Kevin, just remember: the truth shall set you free.' Well, guess what, Mom? You turned out to be right."

She got it. She understood why I needed to tell the truth about my life, so that I could live as an honest and complete person. She went on to found the first chapter of Parents, Families, and Friends of Lesbians and Gays (P-FLAG) in the state of North Carolina. This experience reminded me of the power of truth and its role in changing the hearts and minds of people who have been taught to fear those not like themselves.

The day I received Rita Kissen's manuscript for review, I also received a fax of an editorial that appeared in the *Washington Times*. Written by Lou Sheldon, head of a group called the Traditional Values Coalition and long-time foe of equality for gay people, this editorial, entitled "Classroom Scenario for Coming Out Day," presented a "nightmare" vision for the unsuspecting reader. A confused twelve-year-old is manipulated by a gay teacher, molested by a predatory gay adult, and convinced by a gay counselor to "come out" to his parents. Another victory of recruitment by gays, Sheldon states, and one he warns will soon be coming your way:

> You think this can't happen? This scenario is taken from actual cases in actual public schools across this country. . . . Many parents across this country have no idea with what their children are being indoctrinated, at the most innocent and vulnerable of ages, [because of the infiltration of] the radical homosexual agenda in the public schools.

By inciting the fears and paranoia of parents—who worry, first and foremost, about their children's safety and therefore naturally react with alarm to images of people preying on their kids—Sheldon creates a convincing horror story, one that has enabled him to build a multimillion-dollar organization to combat the "threat" of organizations like GLSTN, which, by contrast, has a budget of less than a quarter-million dollars. There's only one problem with Lou Sheldon's scenario: he's lying.

Rita Kissen tells us the truth.

In Rita's moving and superbly documented book, we learn what really goes on with lesbian, gay, and bisexual teachers. In the place of the predatory monsters created by Sheldon, Kissen paints a picture of dedicated professionals, often torn between their desire to serve their students and their need to be themselves. Kissen shows us the reality of the lives of these teachers who, far from preying on children, often pay an immense personal price because they so desperately want to make life better for the next generation. And she shows us that even in places like Oregon and Colorado—where Sheldon sympathizers have succeeded in staging obscene referendums in which the very humanity of gay people is called into question—these teachers have told their truths and survived. They have replaced ignorance with knowledge, stereotypes with realities, and fear with hope.

In short, they have replaced lies with truths.

Rita Kissen has written a very dangerous book, because telling the truth is always dangerous—and is also the only sure road to safety. As long as people like Sheldon can invoke the myth of the predatory gay teacher, not only gay educators but all gay people are at risk. As long as an entire group of people can be stereotyped as a threat to children, there is little hope that they can be protected from discrimination. And as long as lies like Sheldon's are the only images we have of gay teachers in the public imagination, we stand little chance of convincing people that gays are fit to be educators and, by extension, fit members of society.

Rita's book replaces the cynical, dishonest images purveyed by the Sheldons of the world with true stories and human faces, ones that make it impossible to believe lies again. And it is this truth telling that must take place. As Rita so aptly points out in Chapter 6, mere policies and laws will never keep people safe from discrimination (witness the enormous numbers of closeted teachers in the nine states and innumerable localities where discrimination on the basis of sexual orientation is now illegal). Only the truth will set us free—a truth that shows gay teachers are not the monsters of Sheldon's ravings but are instead caring, dedicated, and competent professionals.

That's the truth Rita tells. And it is an enormous gift, one that will provide gay teachers with the map and instructions I didn't have when I entered education ten years ago and that will help our straight friends begin to understand who we really are.

Gotta hand it to those P-FLAG Moms like Rita Kissen and Alice Jennings, with that truth-telling thing. They seem to be on to something.

Kevin Jennings
Executive Director, The Gay, Lesbian, and Straight Teachers Network
(GLSTN)
New York City

Acknowledgments

MY FIRST DEBT IS TO THE TEACHERS, COUNSELORS, LIBRARIANS, and administrators who have shared their stories with me. The fact that I cannot identify them all by name is a painful reminder of why I felt the need to write this book in the first place.

Many people offered friendship and hospitality as I traveled around the country talking with teachers. Michelle Serries provided lodging and great conversation in Denver. Ruth Frobe and D. J. Reed helped me feel at home in Seattle. Bill Bigelow and Linda Christensen fed and housed me and helped me connect with gay teachers in Portland, Oregon. Greg Varner gave me an insider's look at Colorado Springs and treated me to the most elegant evening of my research. Laurie Mandel helped connect me with gay teachers on Long Island, and escorted me to the best lunch in Islandia. Linda and her friends invited me to central Maine at a time when I had never traveled beyond Portland and the book was still only an idea. For other connections, direct and indirect, I am grateful to Angela Bowen, Michelle Brodsky (ASL interpreter extraordinaire), Margi Duncombe, Jan Goodman, Jean and Jim Genasci, Denise Hoffner (the bicoastal networking queen), Bruce Loeffler, Paula Stockholm, and Susan Tyler.

Lisa Barnett and Vicki Kasabian have been enthusiastic and helpful editors and ideal advisers in my first book-length venture.

Sindee Gozansky provided prompt and unfailingly accurate transcriptions throughout the three years of this project.

Many friends and colleagues offered helpful advice and were sympathetic listeners while I researched and wrote this book. Thanks to Agnes Bushell, Debby Keyes, Nona Lyons, Diana Long, Howard Solomon, and

Beverly Tatum for encouragement, good ideas, and reassurance. Thanks to the Three Neighbors, Scott, Stormy, and Fred, for keeping me well fed and serenaded. Thank you, David, for all the music that still lives on.

I have learned a great deal about teaching and learning from my colleagues in the Extended Teacher Education Program at the University of Southern Maine, who genuinely care for all their students. Dean Richard Barnes of the College of Education and Human Development is an administrator and friend who models the kind of leadership we all want and need. My soul sisters in the Old Women's Lunch Group shared much laughter, encouragement, and youthful energy. The lesbian and gay communities of Peaks Island and Portland, Maine, have showed me the way life should be and made me feel at home from the moment I arrived. Thanks also to the Portland, Maine, chapter of Parents, Families, and Friends of Lesbians and Gays for providing enduring love and support.

Carole Johnson and the staff at Equity Institute offered inspiration and encouragement; Mare and Laurie Wallace and the Maine Equity team helped bring Project Empowerment to Portland and remain unfailing allies to the gay and lesbian community of Maine.

The Associates at the Maine chapter of the National Coalition Building Institute, under the leadership of Jan Froehlich and Diane Gilman, have taught me more than I can say about changing minds and hearts and have nourished my spirit with their love and friendship.

Kevin Jennings, who graciously agreed to write the foreword for this book, is an inspiration to all teachers and activists, straight and gay. I am proud to be a part of the fledgling Maine chapter of GLSTN, the Gay, Lesbian, and Straight Teachers Network, and to be working with Kevin in this wonderful organization.

Part of the research for this book was made possible by grants from the University of Southern Maine Faculty Senate, the College of Education Faculty Development Committee, and the USM Women's Studies Program. I am grateful to my colleagues on these committees for funding lesbian and gay research at a time of budget cuts and other incursions on academic freedom.

Most of all, I offer my love and appreciation to the members of my blended and extended family, who have lived with this book almost as long as I have: my parents, Goldie and Isidore Kissen, who first told me the story of the Danish King, the Jewish people, and the yellow star; my Great and Terrific children—Michelle, my guide through the wonderful world of women who love women, and Andrew, my favorite hiking and camping partner, who knows what it means to be an ally; Denise, my newest daughter, whose warmth and humor have gladdened our family; and my other children, Mich and André, and their families, who have all made my life richer through their presence. Finally, to Norm, who grows the best garden in the world, thank you for brightening my life with so much love.

Peaks Island, Maine
December 1995

"It's my last closet. And I don't think I'll feel one hundred percent okay until I don't have closets in my life. That would be my ultimate dream."

"Michael," *high school teacher, Oregon*

Introduction

WHEN I WAS TEACHING HIGH SCHOOL IN THE 1970S, A woman on our physical education staff was fired for "unprofessional conduct" involving a female student. The girl's father, who also happened to be the head of the P. E. department, accused "Tina" of seducing his daughter; Tina maintained that all she had done was to talk with a lonely girl who was alienated from her parents. Most of the teachers who knew Tina (and her boss) believed her.

No one would ever have heard Tina's side of the story if a colleague had not happened to wander into her classroom one day after school and find her in tears. Being a compassionate man, he convinced Tina to fight back against the attempt to dismiss her, and offered to contact our local union representative. When the school board ruled in favor of the department head, dozens of students and parents rallied to Tina's defense, and the union rep said he believed she had a legal case worth pursuing. Tina replied that although teaching was all she had ever wanted to do, she could not file a grievance. Articles might be written in newspapers. Details of the story might reach the city where her parents lived—her parents, who did not know she was a lesbian. She thanked the students and teachers who had supported her, collected her books and equipment, and on Monday she was gone. Later, I heard that she had found a job at a local drivers-training school. As far as I know, she never taught high school again.

There was another lesbian at my school, a bright and well-loved teacher. Everyone knew that she lived out in the country with a woman who taught in another district, and that they had a big garden where they raised most of their food. As far as I can remember, neither the teacher nor her colleagues ever used the word "partner" or "lover." They were just "Cindy" and "Lynn," who lived together.

In 1982, my children and I were among the hundreds of thousands—organizers said there were one million of us—who traveled to New York City to participate in the march for nuclear disarmament. When I learned that Cindy and Lynn were planning to go, I invited them to spend the night with us and avoid the long drive to town where we would board the buses in the morning. It was a festive evening; we were full of exhilaration at the approaching end of the school year and the next day's great event. Cindy and Lynn entertained us with stories of the people in their small farming community, but they never once talked of their life together as a couple, nor did we ask. When the hour grew late, I opened the sofa bed in our living room and said I hoped they'd be comfortable. It was the first time all evening that I'd felt awkward, as if I were breaking the taboo of silence around their lives as lesbians.

Back then, I knew that what had happened to Tina was unfair. And I knew that it was wrong for Cindy to have to separate her life as a lesbian woman in a loving relationship from her life as a teacher and a colleague. I even knew that some lesbians and gay men were fighting back against the silence. What I did not know was that my family and I would soon become involved in those struggles, and that the lives of gay and lesbian educators would become part of my life.

Ten years ago, my daughter came out as a lesbian and left home for college. Since then, she has completed a graduate education program and successfully survived her first two years as a high school English teacher, wrestling all the while with the conflict between safety and authenticity that troubles all gay educators. Sharing this process is probably the closest a heterosexual observer can come to the dangers and rewards that lesbian, gay, and bisexual teachers face every day of their working lives. And, as thousands of heterosexual mothers and fathers have discovered, learning that one is the parent of a gay child transforms homophobia and heterosexism from a distant political issue into something immediate, personal, and urgent.

In my professional life as a teacher educator, I have met hundreds of school teachers. Most are people I know only through our limited academic relationship, yet over the years, a steady progression of them have come out to me. Sometimes the disclosure took place in their classrooms, momentarily emptied of students. Sometimes it was at a conference, or a diversity workshop. Although my public involvement in Parents, Families, and Friends of Lesbians and Gays (P-FLAG) and in local gay politics identified me as an ally, the teachers and I knew that revealing their sexual orientation within a professional setting was potentially dangerous. While gay men and lesbians may be growing more visible in American life, teachers who come out in school still risk harassment, dismissal, and physical violence. Yet the gay teachers I have met—from my daughter's graduate school friends to seasoned veterans nearing retirement—all want to come out. They want their colleagues and students to know them as they really are, and they want to live free from the paralyzing demands of hiding.

Four years ago, I began talking with lesbian and gay teachers in a more systematic way, with the idea of turning these conversations into something permanent. I wanted gay teachers, especially those in closeted, isolated places, to know that they were not alone, and to meet some of their gay and lesbian colleagues, if only in the pages of a book. Even more, I wanted heterosexual teachers, school administrators, and parents to hear these voices that have been silenced for too long, and to recognize the poisonous effects of homophobia in schools. As a heterosexual college professor, I knew that I could not presume to speak for lesbian and gay teachers. Instead, I wanted to use my own relative privilege to give them the opportunity to speak in safety and to tell their stories to people who might otherwise never hear them.

The stories in this book come from over a hundred lesbian, gay, and bisexual women and men who are or have been school teachers, counselors, social workers, librarians, and administrators. They teach in nineteen states, in every region of the country, and represent public and private education from preschool to senior high. Although some of the interviews were done over the phone, the great majority (88 out of 105) took place in person.

Hearing lesbian and gay teachers talk about themselves, I soon realized that sexual orientation was only one part—though a crucial one—of their identity. Race and ethnicity, culture, socioeconomic class, religion, ability and disability, age, and geographic identification, all gave meaning to the stories I was hearing. In relating these stories, I have tried to avoid presenting a "laundry list" of identities, but have included racial and cultural identifications when they seemed relevant to the material at hand. Writing about race, especially, I have tried to keep in mind Henry Louis Gates' admonition:

> It's important to remember that "race" is *only* a sociopolitical category, nothing more. At the same time—in terms of its practical peformative force—that doesn't help me when I'm trying to get a taxi on the corner of 125th and Lenox Avenue. ("Please, sir, it's only a metaphor.")[1]

---

[1] Henry Louis Gates, *Loose Canons: Notes on the Culture Wars* (New York: Oxford University Press, 1992), pp. 37–38.

In the same way, I have chosen not to enter into the debate over language and identity within the gay community—the tensions between "gay/lesbian/bisexual," and "queer," for example, or the question of whether there is, in fact, such a thing as a homosexual/gay/queer identity. Here again, I find Gates helpful.

> Foucault says . . . that the "homosexual" as life form was invented sometime in the mid-nineteenth century. Now, if there's no such thing as a homosexual, then homophobia, at least as directed toward people rather than acts, loses its rationale. But you can't respond to the discrimination against gay people by saying, "I'm sorry, I don't exist; you've got the wrong guy." The simple historical fact is, Stonewall was necessary, concerted action was necessary to take action against the very structures that, as it were, called the homosexual into being, that subjected certain people to this imaginary identity.[2]

In the day-to-day lives of gay teachers, it doesn't matter much whether homosexuality is an identity, a set of behaviors, an essential inborn characteristic, or a chosen "life-style." What matters is that vast numbers of dedicated teachers do not feel safe in school, for reasons that have nothing to do with their merit as educators.

Some of the teachers in this book are personal friends and acquaintances who volunteered to share their stories as soon as they heard about the project. Others responded to ads in gay newspapers or flyers at education conferences. Some learned about the book and contacted me directly. Indeed, one of my great discoveries has been the eagerness of lesbian and gay teachers to tell their stories. I believe this eagerness reflects a deep desire for authenticity, for in all my conversations with gay teachers, I have never met one who did not want to be out in school. Like heterosexual teachers, gay educators want the world to know them as full human beings.

When it came to names, I invited teachers to identify themselves in any way they wished. Some wanted to use their own first names or full names; others preferred to use a pseudonym of their own choosing, or asked me to choose one for them. I have indicated pseudonyms with quotation marks the first time a name is mentioned.

Writing this book has been the most rewarding experience of my teaching career. Again and again, I was moved by the warmth and generosity of teachers who welcomed me into their lives, and in many cases into their

[2] *Ibid.*, p. 38.

homes and communities. From an impromptu pizza party in Seattle to a quiet cup of tea in a Boston kitchen, from a defiant Gay Pride march in post–Amendment Two Colorado to a neighborly lesbian reunion in rural Maine, the people in this book have made me part of their family, and have given me gifts beyond measure. I hope what I have written is worthy of their courage.

PART ONE

The Center of Myself

"I always saw teaching as an extension of other things
that are really at the center of myself."

"Peggy," *high school teacher, Maine*

1

Becoming a Teacher

ASK ANY GROUP OF EDUCATORS WHY THEY CHOSE TEACHING, and they will tell a few familiar stories. They may remember a remarkable grade school teacher who made math or history come alive. They will probably mention a love for children, and a desire to share something they care about with others, whether it is Shakespearean drama or the finer points of tennis. Though they may initially enter teaching as a "safe" career with job security and summer vacations, most educators who stay in the profession love what they do and want to make a difference in the lives of young people.

Lesbian and gay teachers face a host of challenges, from figuring out how to conceal their gay identity to finding safe ways to confront homophobia. Whether they are completely closeted, completely out, or somewhere in between, their lives are complicated by stresses of which most of their heterosexual colleagues are completely unaware. Yet when they talk about being teachers, lesbian and gay educators sound remarkably like everybody else. Like Curt, a high school teacher in Colorado, they "enjoy seeing a light come on in a kid's head." And like audiovisual director Thomas Juul, they thrive on emotional and intellectual interaction with young people.

> I love kids crawling on me. . . . I can have more fun in twenty minutes of working with a kid. . . . I sit down and read with them and talk to them about it. . . . I love being able to be creative. I love throwing paint on the windows in my library, which I do. I paint the windows every month. I have the kids wash them off and they paint the slogan of the month. I put displays up all over the building. . . . I love it.

Karen Cosper, a Portland, Oregon, elementary school teacher, started teaching at the age of thirty, after ten years out of school. But she thought of herself as a teacher long before she actually entered the classroom.

> I did some other things for a while. I worked for the post office. I worked in restaurants. I taught aerobics. . . . I traveled, I moved and lived in different places. . . . [But] even when I worked at the post office, I'd say, "I'm a teacher, but I work at the post office now."

Christopher Rodriguez, director of the Harvey Milk School of the Hetrick-Martin Institute in New York City, came to teaching through his work with incarcerated minors in the Los Angeles County juvenile court system. His idea of himself as a teacher is tied up with his desire to be a doctor some day: "I approach this work from a perspective of healing, and that's kind of how it all makes sense for me."

For Peggy, an urban high school English teacher in Maine, teaching is the identity that brings all her other identities together.

> I always saw teaching as an extension of other things that are really at the center of myself. It's a spiritual activity, it's a very musical activity, it's totally integrated into the deepest places of me.

Like teachers everywhere, gay educators often remember parents or grandparents for whom teaching was more than just a job, and teachers and counselors who inspired and believed in them. "Leslie," a high school social studies teacher who worked in private industry for a while, says she comes "from a long line of teachers—my great-grandmother, my grandmother, and various other people in my family." When she started feeling "a sense of aimlessness," the solution was obvious: "I decided to go back to school."

"Annette," a high school teacher on the West Coast, was inspired by her mother's role in their church.

> I grew up in the Presbyterian church, and when I was ten years old I started working with the younger kids. . . . I think this was modeled after my mother, 'cause she did a lot of work in Christian education . . . and so I started being a teacher of my younger sister and her friends . . . and took them to the park and did things with them.

For "Lourdes," a first-generation Filipina now teaching middle school in California, becoming a teacher was a way of defying rather than fulfilling her family's expectations. Though her parents wanted her to become a doctor, she soon discovered that she "didn't want to be around sick people."

When her college roommate began a teacher education program during their sophomore year, Lourdes realized: "It was the only thing I could ever imagine myself doing. It was just suddenly the right thing."

Many gay teachers associate a career in education with the desire to help others. "Hope," now a school social worker at a Long Island junior high school, was "the Ann Landers of all my friends." "Claire," a Maine elementary school counselor, switched from teaching to counseling after working with adults who had dropped out of school. "I came to have a real appreciation of the [role] that self-esteem plays in people's aspirations," she says.

"Mary," a hearing teacher at a school for the Deaf, began to envision herself as a nurturer during her childhood in New Jersey.

> I grew up near a school for the Deaf . . . and I used to go there sledding in the wintertime—they had a big hill. I saw the kids signing and that fascinated me. Then I also had the opportunity to watch "The Miracle Worker.". . . I used to set my dolls up and set up a classroom with my little play chalkboard, but then as I got older I thought that I wanted something even more challenging in teaching.

The story of how Annie Sullivan taught young deaf-and-blind Helen Keller the meaning of language has captured the imagination of many teachers, both straight and gay, who dream of working miracles in young hearts and minds. For California high school teacher Terry Minton, who grew up denying his gayness in rural Oklahoma, the film is more troubling.

> I think probably it was kind of an Annie Sullivan complex, you know . . . what I really wanted was to be the miracle worker. . . . And looking back on that . . . I realize now that the idea of sacrificing your life to make someone else's life possible has enormous appeal when you don't much value your own life—your own existence.

But most gay teachers have happier memories. Cary, a special education teacher in a Dallas elementary school, recalls his childhood in a Texas town of two thousand as a time when "school was a huge part of my life . . . [I was] involved in a lot of activities. . . . I guess there just was never a question as to what it was I wanted to do."

Rhoda, a former elementary school teacher who grew up in suburban Long Island, was equally at home in the classroom.

> I loved school. . . . I was in love with my second-grade teacher. . . . She just let me read books the whole day. . . . And sometimes she would let me sit in

front of the classroom and lead the reading class. You know, pick on kids to read and make sure they read correctly.

Many share Rhoda's affectionate memory of a special teacher or coach, and some gay teachers interpret these same-sex crushes as signs of a developing sexual orientation that they understand only in retrospect. Karen, a Maine junior high school teacher, was married for twenty years before coming out as a lesbian; yet in her recollection of an admired junior high school teacher she hints that she was a lesbian long before she knew it:

> I think the reason I'm a teacher is because in seventh and eighth grade I fell in love with my French teacher. . . . I remember the crushing blow I felt when I found out she was married. . . . I loved how this woman looked, and I loved how she moved, and I loved what she wore, and she was just wonderful, and I thought, Oh, my God, she's married, how could she do that? So I became a French teacher.

Patricia Tomaso acknowledges that she decided to teach physical education because of "the only person I could identify with, that I thought somehow [was] simpatico with me . . . my gym teacher, who was gay and who's a good friend now."

But not all role models were same-sex teachers. "Jeff," who teaches at a Catholic school in Maine, was influenced by "a really fantastic biology teacher. . . . I was kind of [on] the college track, but even with the kids who weren't, everybody loved her. 'Cause she really cared."

And Dianne, a Maine middle school teacher, remembers being "in love" with her freshman high school English teacher: "That passion sort of set the stage for my own being an English teacher. He probably knew I had this huge crush on him but he was just wonderful."

Gay and lesbian teachers of color, and members of other cultural minorities, recall educators who helped them develop a positive ethnic or cultural identity. Torey, an African American history teacher in suburban Chicago, remembers a counselor who inspired him when he was growing up in Galveston, Texas.

> I felt uncomfortable being in some of the honors classes and I wanted to move down. He wouldn't allow me to do it. He pretty much forced my hand and said, "You're going to stick it out." And he already had determined that I was going to college, and he was going to get all these scholarships for me.

When he began thinking about teaching as a career, Torey recalled other positive role models who had inspired him.

> People were telling me how my presence was needed in the classroom as an African American male. . . . And I really took that under serious consideration, looking back on my life and how I had so many African American role models that I could rely on through my growing up, and how that may not be the case in many communities.

Steph Sforza, a Deaf lesbian who now works as a teacher's aide at a school for the Deaf, felt that she needed to be the same kind of role model for Deaf students.

> I grew up in a Deaf residential school. . . . Most of my elementary and junior high school teachers were hearing [but] I had a Deaf social studies teacher and I had a Deaf math teacher. So I really looked up to those teachers . . . I wanted to feel like I could look at those Deaf teachers and see my language and my culture.

For women growing up in the 1950s and 1960s, teaching was often more an expectation than a choice, so it is not surprising that many lesbian teachers in their forties and fifties were directed into education as an "acceptable" career. "Lynn," an early-intervention specialist in rural Maine, wanted to go to veterinary school, but was pressured into a teaching degree instead. Jan Goodman graduated from high school in 1969, and has worked in Massachusetts and California as an elementary school teacher, administrator, and museum educator. "The options for girls were very limited, and teaching always appealed to me 'cause I always liked little kids. But I think that had it been now, I probably would have become a journalist."

Deann LeBeau, a Connecticut high school teacher nearing retirement, learned in high school that she had three choices as a young woman.

> You could be a secretary, you could be a nurse, or you could be a teacher. . . . And I didn't like blood and stuff so I couldn't be a nurse, and I didn't think I could sit still long enough to be a secretary, so I guessed I was gonna be a teacher.

The same message was directed at Shirley, a high school math teacher who grew up in the Midwest.

> You could be a teacher. You could be a nurse. You could be a secretary. You could go work at the factory. . . . Boys if they were good in mathematics could be engineers. Girls could be teachers.

Lesbians and gay men who entered teaching from other professions had to adjust to a world where they needed to hide their gay identity, in some cases more completely than in their previous careers. But in deciding to become teachers, they thought more about meaning and values than about the risks of being gay or lesbian. "Ruth," who worked in a corporate office before becoming an elementary school teacher, liked the "safeness and comfort and nurturance" of the teaching profession. Philip Robinson, who coordinates student support services at an inner-city Boston middle school, became a counselor after a year as an English teacher because he felt he could benefit the students better "by having a closer rapport, one-on-one" with them.

Nancy is a Deaf teacher at an elementary school for the Deaf on the East Coast. She became a teacher after studying accounting at Gallaudet University and working in business.

> I realized the office was really the hearing world, and I wanted to be with the Deaf community. . . . I volunteered in the Peace Corps and that kind of made me want to be a teacher. . . . The communication was there, the language was there, everything was there, and I realized Deaf children need Deaf teachers. . . . It's like, you know, if I want to become a teacher I have to work with Deaf children.

Like many straight teachers, some gay educators entered the profession for less-than-idealistic reasons—the need for security, or a sense that they weren't sure what else they wanted to do. "Paul," a thirteen-year veteran who teaches high school in northern Virginia, originally chose teaching as "an immediately marketable way" to pursue his interest in languages. Lyn Boudreau, a Colorado music teacher whose creative energy has made her a favorite among students and parents, admits that she "fell into" teaching "out of needing security." Deborah Schwartz, who has taught literature and writing in a variety of alternative settings in New York, wryly reflects that she "fell into teaching to make money to support my writing habit. Which is ironic 'cause I haven't found a way to make enough money off of it."

But no matter how pragmatic their initial reasons, lesbian and gay teachers who have remained in the profession have found that teaching is more than just a job.

"I ended up going into education sort of by default," admits Timothy Brown, a Denver high school teacher. "I wasn't all that interested in it at first. Then as I took more course work and got out doing practicum experiences with real live children in different settings, I got really enthusiastic and excited."

Alejandra Dubove, an independent school teacher born in Argentina and raised in Texas, majored in history and English. She got a teaching certificate as "a safety net, in case I couldn't find a job." But once she started student teaching, she discovered that it was the only career she wanted.

> What a great job, I thought, because you're being paid for reading and learning and working with kids, and every day you're learning something new. . . . You're not sitting at a desk, you get all this interaction, new ideas, and you get to be really creative. If you love drama, you can do drama in class. If you love to write, or be poetic, you have all these opportunities.

Pam, a high school computer teacher, found her way to teaching through coaching. "I always enjoyed working with kids . . . I really liked sports and was into coaching and the easiest way to be involved in coaching is to be in education." "Sue," another coach-turned-teacher who now teaches middle school in Oregon, had been involved in track and cross-country during her own school years. "I started coaching at a junior high . . . and really loved working with the kids. It was so much fun I decided that I wanted to get my teaching certification."

Like all good teachers, lesbian and gay educators associate teaching with sharing what they love most. "Joseph," a new teacher just completing his undergraduate preparation, says being a teacher is like taking his cousins bird-watching and "feeling so good that they're amazed by it and that they can learn something by it." Michelle Serries, a former Denver middle school teacher, found the door to teaching through a directing job in children's theatre, where she decided that she was "meant to teach even though I swore I would never do it because both my parents were teachers and I didn't want to follow in their footsteps." For "Jessie," a high school science teacher on the North Shore of Long Island, teaching is tied to "the whole purpose of science . . . to question everything you see and ask why . . . passing on the questions, not the answers."

Why, then, do lesbians and gay men become teachers? For the same reasons that straight people do. They care about children. They love ideas, or a particular field of knowledge. And somewhere along the way, they discover that they are good at sharing what they know with others. Lesbians and gay men become teachers for all the best reasons in the world, reasons that have nothing to do with their sexual orientation. Only when they encounter the pressures of homophobia—the fear and hatred of gay people—does being a teacher become a problem.

2

Discovering a Gay Identity

TO BE A LESBIAN OR GAY TEACHER, IN MOST SCHOOLS, IS TO walk a constant line between safety and honesty. Like all good teachers, gay and lesbian educators want to be open and authentic with their students and colleagues. They want to trust and be trusted, to cultivate the "I-Thou" relationship that Martin Buber describes as the basis of education. At the same time, gay teachers know that in most places they can be fired, harassed, or even physically assaulted if they are honest about their sexual orientation. The very qualities of trust and authenticity that lie at the heart of all good teaching are often incompatible with their physical and emotional well-being. Teachers who know they are gay before they enter the profession must consider what that identity will mean for them as educators; those who come out after they have already begun teaching find this new identity a threat in an environment where they have always felt at home. Either way, acknowledging a gay identity means rethinking the whole notion of being a teacher. Ron, a Portland, Oregon, high school teacher, recalls:

> When I came out, it was really, really a wonderful time, but also a really scary time. And a lot of questioning about whether I should stay in education . . . because I felt in lots of ways I was on a collision course if I stayed in education, with some real problems down the line. But then on the other hand I felt, well maybe I had something really special to offer. And I think I'm on that fence for the last ten years. It's been . . . scary, it's been exciting, satisfying, it's been horrendous, it's been all those things.

Daniel Dromm, who now teaches fourth grade in Queens, New York, abandoned his original plan to be a high school Spanish teacher; he feared that he would be unable to discipline teenagers "because . . . of the problem of them realizing that I was gay. And then I would lose control of the class and not be able to teach." "Bill," an elementary school principal in Colorado, wondered how he would be "perceived as a gay man being a principal," and decided that he "would never lie . . . but would probably never tell the entire truth as an openly gay man."

"Rodney" is a former teacher who worked for years at a large Christian school in Colorado. Because of the school's fundamentalist principles, Rodney decided he had to resign when he finally acknowledged his sexual orientation. He feels a great deal of sadness when he thinks of the colleagues he left behind, most of whom will never know who he really is.

> I guess it was primarily my desire to share my life with someone I loved, and if that meant that I had to quit that job to be able to do that without creating a big public hullabaloo with the school, then that's what I decided to do. . . . I loved those people I worked with at that school. . . . They were excellent educators, they were just wonderful people. I enjoyed being with my colleagues so much, and that's one thing I missed really strongly.

Not all teachers conclude that they must leave teaching in order to be gay. But all are affected by societal attitudes about lesbians and gay men working with children. Sometimes the messages come from sources close to home. "Frank" now teaches junior high school in Puyallup, Washington. When he first announced his plans to become a teacher, his family refused to pay his college tuition.

> I think my family knew that I was gay and then tried to convince me to maybe look at other options. . . . So I dropped out of college my senior year and I went and lived in Israel for a year on the West Bank. . . . [I] met an Israeli and came out.

When he returned home, determined to be a teacher after all, Frank's father was still unsympathetic.

> We never talked about it, but every time something was gonna happen, he'd say, "Remember, you're a teacher now." A friend of mine was coming to visit from Kansas City and he said, "Remember." I was gonna pick him up at the airport, and he goes, "Remember, you're a teacher now." And I looked at him and I said, "What do you think? I'm gonna rape him in the airport? I mean it's just a friend of mine coming to visit." But he wouldn't

talk about it and he wouldn't accept it and he wouldn't admit it, but he just kept on reminding me, "Remember, you're a teacher."

Other gay teachers remember similar warnings from mentors and professors. D. J. Reed, a Kentwood, Washington, high school teacher, was cautioned by one of her college instructors "never to say anything about who I spent my time with." Her friend Ruth Frobe remembers hearing a professor tell another woman in her undergraduate program, "If you expect to teach P. E. in a public school, you need to shave your legs."

Ruth's comment raises the specter of the "butch" lesbian who walks down the street dressed in heavy shoes and work pants, has a short haircut, and plays in a softball league. Like most stereotypes, this one is both true and false. It belies the great diversity of lesbian identities, but it also reflects the fact that many lesbians do, in fact, find traditional female clothing confining and uncomfortable. So do many straight women. In fact, there is no more graphic way to illustrate the connection between homophobia and sexism than to observe how quickly any woman who dresses and behaves in "unfeminine" ways can be labeled a lesbian.

Within the charged atmosphere of a school, these complex attitudes and stereotypes take on incredible intensity, as adolescent boys and girls grapple with their sexuality and struggle to fulfil—or defy—socially prescribed roles. Not surprising, the person most likely to become the lightening rod for all this anxiety is the lesbian coach or P. E. teacher. Her interest in sports, and often her appearance, confirm the "butch" stereotype; yet at the same time, they represent an alternative to traditional "feminine" expectations, an alternative she—and her lesbian students—may find extremely liberating.

"Ellen," a high school social studies teacher, coached women's lacrosse after college and pursued a teaching degree with the idea of becoming a P. E. teacher. But she soon switched to history. "I've had several friends who are P. E. teachers who are gay," she explains, "and they take a great deal of abuse. I don't know if I would have gone into teaching if that had been my field."

"Julie" began her career wanting to teach P. E., and did so for a while before switching to high school math. "My dad would not even sign my college application," she recalls. "When he would talk about me, I was 'a teacher.' . . . When I switched to math, then I was 'a math teacher.' He wouldn't say, 'She's a P. E. teacher.'"

"Jody," a junior high school teacher who stayed in P. E., heard the same message from her father, but thought fast enough to retaliate. "My dad had said to me, I don't know how many times, 'You can be anything you want but

don't be a P. E. teacher, 'cause they're a bunch of fat dykes with big asses.' . . .
And I told him, 'I'm never gonna get fat, Dad.'"

Faced with so many difficulties, why do lesbians and gay men pursue their
desire to teach? For many, like Jody, the presence of other gay teachers reas-
sures them that they can survive.

> We were always together and we were always best friends, and we were all
> going into the same thing . . . and so I just thought, you know . . . like a
> million people have done it before me and before them, and you know,
> we're gonna last.

> Alan Kelly-Hamm's first job in education was in day-care, where "all the
> gay men I knew worked . . . if they had any consciousness at all." Annette
> worked at a preschool in a low-income neighborhood, where "a lot of the
> staff were gay and some of the mothers who had kids at our center were gay,
> and so we were pretty out to most of the families."
> Bob Bradley, who teaches junior high school on Long Island, drew his
> early support from a graduate instructor in a human sexuality course he took
> shortly after coming out. The course required a final project, and the instruc-
> tor gave Bob a very specific assignment.

> He called me in and said he never, ever assigned projects to anybody, but to
> me he was. He said, "You're gay, and you're so deep in the closet you need
> to come out. And so my assignment to you is, you are required to go to
> three gay bars."

Bob fulfilled the assignment, and found it "fascinating." On his first visit, he
brought a straight colleague, "for protection," but on his second visit, he went
alone.

> To my great shock and terror, I noticed a colleague, another teacher from
> the district, in this gay bar. Oh my God, what do I do? And I quickly real-
> ized, what am I worried about? He's here. And that was my introduction,
> really, to making gay friends.

Once they actually enter the classroom, gay teachers are glad to find
other lesbians and gay men in their schools. "Valerie" and her partner moved
to Portland, Oregon, from South Dakota, where they had been almost
entirely closeted. Shortly afterward, Valerie began teaching middle school,

and was happy to find "this whole underground network where people know who else is lesbian and gay at that school."

Still, many young lesbians and gay men enter teaching unprepared for the extent to which homophobia will rule their lives. "I think I was real naive," says Carolyn, a Michigan social studies teacher. "I didn't understand that if they don't like you because you're a lesbian, there are other things that they could do to threaten your job, and probably would do." Linda, whose first teaching job was at a small junior high in Maine, admits, "I didn't have any conception what kind of toll it would take on me to work at a place that was that rural and that difficult."

Lyn Boudreau spent ten years in the protected environment of a Catholic convent before coming out as a lesbian and leaving religious life. When she entered the world of public school teaching, she experienced homophobia all at once. "I didn't know a lot of the homophobic hatred out there. It was like waking up one morning and realizing you're Black. . . . It's just, 'Oh my gosh, there's people that hate me because I am a lesbian.'"

But even teachers who have been out in the world do not always anticipate the difficulties they will face as gay educators. Paul, who has heard his share of homophobic remarks at his high school, admits, "I thought about it, but not very much. I probably would think about it more now, knowing what I know." "Gwen" says she has not been targeted by her seventh graders, but adds on reflection, "I think if I had really thought it through, I probably wouldn't have done it."

The negative stereotypes are hardest for those who are still uncomfortable about their gay identity. Joseph, who acknowledges that he is still coming to terms with the conflict between his Catholic upbringing and his gayness, is troubled by the image of the teacher as moral exemplar.

> As a teacher, I've always lived my life as an example of how I'd like people to live their lives. . . . I discourage my students from acting up . . . how can I do that when I'm gay, you know? . . . I guess I look at it like I'm acting up too 'cause . . . it's so ingrained in me that it's not a right thing to be.

For lesbians and gay men who come out after they are already teaching, the problem is not whether to be a teacher, but how to incorporate this new identity into the lives they have already constructed. Claire had been a school counselor for three years when she fell in love with her best friend. For a year, she lived "a compartmentalized life" in her small Maine community.

> I had this very strong emotional and physically intimate relationship with this woman who lived in the same town and whose kids were in my schools.

We both went to the same church, in fact we taught Sunday school together. But I never let that part of my life flow into the rest of my life. Well, what does this mean for the rest of my life? It was pretty stressful, pretty paranoid.

Rodney, too, lived a divided life at his Christian school, until he was forced to acknowledge his gay identity.

I didn't know anybody that was gay until I was in my thirties, and I didn't know that there was a possibility of finding someone to love in the way that my whole being told me I needed to love. . . . I tried not to think about it, and as long as nobody preached it from the pulpit or spoke about it in chapel, they didn't bother me too much.

Like others who have come out midway into their teaching careers, Rodney initially found his wife and child "the perfect front. . . . I was married and I had a daughter, and she went to that school and everybody knew that she was my daughter. So I kind of lived behind that."

Divorced or widowed gay teachers, especially if they have children by their previous marriages, find similar protection. Doyle Forister, who came out after his wife died, said his gay identity "didn't affect the teaching career. Everybody in school knew that I was straight because I had been married. . . . Nobody suspected anything."

Unmarried teachers, on the other hand, often find that no matter how closeted they try to remain, coming out changes the way they are treated in school. Dianne was twenty-nine when she realized she was a lesbian. Coming out changed the way others saw her, even though she never disclosed her sexual identity at school.

All the years that I taught in Tennessee I didn't have to deal with homophobia. It's kind of weird though, because . . . I'm still the same person now as I was then. But I guess it was just a little mental switch that I hadn't flipped in my head. So the people I dealt with, it hadn't flipped for them either. They probably thought of me as this sexless person, which I was. I was just going along being a teacher. Then I moved to Maine, and that's when things started to come together and that's when I started having problems . . . covert attacks from kids like notes left on the bathroom walls.

Nancy Goldstein, a former school social worker, says of herself: "I don't think I come across like a straight woman. I have a different energy, you know, and I think people pick up on that—even if they're not aware of it."

As they struggle to integrate their new gay identities into their established teaching identities, most lesbian and gay teachers ultimately find this "different energy" a source of strength. Rebecca was a married high school English teacher in Wyoming when she came out, divorced her husband, and moved to the East Coast. Acknowledging her lesbian identity changed her teaching along with the rest of her life. "I saw myself starting . . . to become more issue concerned. Not just gay-lesbian issues but issues of life. I don't know—but somebody finally turned a light on that said, these things concern you."

Like Rebecca, Ruth values her lesbian identity as a positive part of her life. "It has allowed my mind to think in diverse, creative ways, which I think is an important element in being a teacher."

To Pam, teaching as a lesbian means empathizing with students who are targeted or oppressed. To illustrate, she recalls an anecdote from a workshop she attended.

> A man was talking about some guy who came to him and said that he loved him, and the man said, "Do you know my pain?" and the other guy said, "No, I don't know what pains you," and the man said, "You can't love me until you know what hurts me, what my pain is."

Although gay educators agree that it is difficult to be a lesbian or gay teacher, those who lived through the invisibility of the pre-Stonewall years see life getting easier for their younger gay colleagues, and many of the younger colleagues concur. Pat Tomaso, a retired Chicago P. E. teacher and playground supervisor, recalls a "really scary" moment during her first year of teaching, when someone in the gay community threatened to expose her sexual orientation "because I didn't accept a date or something. They just said, 'Well, what if we called the board of education and told them that you're a lesbian.' I don't even remember what the circumstances were, but I just remember the terror that was in my heart." Pat "got brave enough" to ask one of her supervisors what would happen if someone did call, and received assurances that the board of education "would never take any kind of statement made by an anonymous person seriously. . . . So I trusted that information." Asked if that made her feel better, Pat replies, "a little bit—but, no."

Hearing this story from someone who began her teaching career before he was born, Pat's friend David Larson is moved by the contrast to his own life.

> It just amazes me how different our stories are. Being in Madison [where he went to college] was probably the best place for me to come out, 'cause I knew for three or four years that there was a help line and there's lots of support for gay students. . . . I'm almost worried that I'm too relaxed at

school. My parents are very concerned that they wouldn't want to keep me on staff if they knew, but our principal is incredibly supportive and gay friendly.

Ultimately, every gay or lesbian teacher must find his or her own way to integrate "gay" and "educator" into one coherent identity. Those torn by the contradictions might consider Karen Cosper's words as she describes her life during Oregon's two antigay referendum campaigns.

Earlier, I thought . . . if only I wasn't wanting to be a teacher I could become involved in some of these things. . . . And if I had another occupation, boy, then I could really get involved. . . . But when we started feeling backed up against the wall with the Oregon Citizens Alliance, it kind of all came together. It's like I knew I was a lesbian before I was a teacher and I'd be one after I was a teacher. It was the thing that was with me really to stay, and I felt that I had to be true to that first.

3

Race and Culture

BEVERLY TATUM, A SCHOLAR AND ACTIVIST WHO HAS WRIT-
ten extensively about racial identity, describes an exercise in which she asks
her students to produce as many responses as possible to the words "I
am . . ." According to Beverly, what is revealing about the results is not what
participants include, but what they leave out. Women often write "I am a
woman"; men rarely write "I am male," or "I am a man." People of color
usually write "I am African American," or "I am Latino," but few participants
write "I am White." And while those who feel safe enough to disclose a gay
identity may write, "I am lesbian," "I am gay," or "I am bisexual," few people
write, "I am heterosexual."

This exercise shows that how we think about our identity comes not
only from our individual experiences but also from our understanding of our
place in the world around us. Men, Euro-Americans, heterosexuals, middle-
class people, do not omit those identities from their self-descriptions because
they are unimportant, but because they are so important that they are taken
for granted. The identities that give us privilege are the "norm" in the wider
society and, unless our life experiences teach us otherwise, they become the
norm in our own thinking too.

Lesbian and gay teachers share one common identity that places them
outside the mainstream of heterosexual society. But, like all gay and lesbian
people, gay teachers are defined by more than their sexual orientation. Race
and ethnicity, ability and disability, age, socioeconomic class, religion, and
gender are all part of who they are as people and as teachers. If they are people of color, they are likely to talk about their struggles to connect their ethnic
identity with their gay identity. If they are members of cultural or religious

minorities, they may make connections between growing up Jewish, or Deaf, or disabled, and growing up gay. Many gay teachers who have known economic hardship connect their experience of being poor with their struggles as lesbians or gay men. In each case, a common thread of oppression runs through the struggle to make sense of identities that often resist integration. Exploring the relationship between homophobia and other oppressions is painful and difficult, but it can also lead to greater empowerment.

For gay and lesbian teachers of color, working in a profession whose members are overwhelmingly White is often as important—in some cases more important—as the struggle to be a gay teacher in a heterosexual world. Thinking back, many remember adults in their ethnic communities who helped them develop a positive identity. Christopher Rodriguez, a second-generation Mexican American, says he came to appreciate his role models only after leaving home.

> One of the things I realized very soon after I left San Antonio, Texas, to go to college in Ithaca, New York, was how privileged I had been to live in a community which was . . . almost 50 percent Latino. . . . We had teachers in my school who were Latino. . . . I had very, very strong family support. . . . All those things were a privilege that I came to really appreciate many years later when I went to a place like Cornell and had a very different experience.

Torey grew up in Galveston, Texas, where life could be confusing, despite the presence of strong African American adults. As a child, he attended a private school, and remembers himself as "a little Black boy walking through the projects in a green plaid uniform." His high school years were "a real dichotomy experience," during which he spent his school days with the White students in his honors classes, while "at home it was nothing but other African Americans." Torey's family environment provided a great deal of encouragement for a young African American man, but little acknowledgment that it was acceptable to be gay. "To this day, it's not even discussed in my family," he says, though he adds that his mother has finally stopped asking him who he is dating.

Others describe the mixture of comfort and conflict that a close-knit ethnic community can present for a young person developing a gay identity. Lourdes grew up among Filipino immigrants in the San Francisco Bay area, and still teaches only one block from her parents' home, in a school that is 28 percent Filipino and 60 percent Asian. She finds this a more comfortable environment than her previous school, which was mostly White, but has a hard time coming out to her Filipino colleagues. "They're connected [with] my parents' community and I kind of feel like I'm trespassing on their territory," she explains. Lourdes was invited to work on a committee addressing homophobia in the mainstream Asian community, but declined. "I can't do that. The Filipino community is so large in this town, you know, I might as well make an announcement, because that would mean I would be out."

Deborah Schwartz grew up in an Orthodox Jewish family ("but not ultra-Orthodox") and has taught African American and Puerto Rican youth in several alternative programs. She found a liberal Hebrew school the hardest place to come out.

> When I really peeled back the layers I felt very close to them. . . . They were leftists too, who looked and sounded a lot more like me than anyone else I'd ever taught. I felt very welcomed to a degree—and to come out to them felt as if I was risking everything.

Deborah knows other women who have found it easier to come out to students outside their own communities.

> I know a lot of White lesbians who teach in Black or Latino or even White working-class neighborhoods, and find it easier than going to where they came from and coming out. . . . I have a good friend who's Puerto Rican, she's bisexual and she was teaching in an organization for Puerto Rican women, a literacy program. The White lesbians wanted to come out, and the Puerto Rican lesbians didn't. The White women ended up coming out.

Homophobia in their home culture is especially painful for lesbian and gay teachers of color as they seek refuge from racism in the White world. Joseph finds it "tough being gay in a Hispanic family." At one time, Catholicism was an important link to his family and community. "I really felt good going to church and singing and being with my family," he says. "But once we come to terms with 'I'm gay,' or 'I'm lesbian,' we feel distant." Joseph adds that he has attended one mass at Dignity, the Catholic lesbian and gay organization, but "it was just a mass." What he really wants is "a support group where you sit down and talk."

Nancy, a Deaf teacher who left the business world to work with Deaf children, still finds the Deaf community "very homophobic," and does not come out to people at Deaf events. "If they ask me, I'll tell them. But . . . I don't trust them." Nancy adds that she doesn't think the Deaf community is any more homophobic than the hearing community, but the pain of rejection is more acute when it comes from family members or Deaf acquaintances. Nancy came out to her mother over the TTY, the device that allows Deaf people to communicate over telephone lines with keyboard and computer screen. At first, her mother refused to discuss the subject. Finally, Nancy confronted her in person. "I said, 'I can't hold this in any more. I need to discuss it.' I cried . . . and she hugged me and from then on it's been better."

Nancy and her mother were able to break through the boundaries that separated them as Deaf lesbian and hearing heterosexual. Her relationship with her father has been very different. "I know my father is very prejudiced against gay people so I haven't told him," she says. "The two of us don't have any communication, so why should I tell him?" Nancy's father has never learned American Sign Language—her language—so that while he is a part of her family, he is not part of her culture. For this reason, she will not share her lesbian identity with him.

Steph Sforza, a Deaf lesbian whose family was more receptive to her coming out than Nancy's, says her Deaf acquaintances are much more interested in where she grew up and what school she attended than in her sexual orientation. She speaks of her primary identity as being Deaf, rather than being a lesbian. "My needs are related to being Deaf. I need a TTY, I need a light on my phone, I need a closed-caption decoder on my TV. So that's my first priority, really."

Other minority teachers agree that their home cultures are less homophobic than mainstream American society. Lourdes believes that her father, who would sometimes use the term "fag" in the days before she came out to him, did not "bring that with him" from the Philippines, but "learned that here." She points out that her mother, who is less assimilated into American culture, is less homophobic and has gay friends at work.

Chris Nunez, a Mexican American educator who coordinates a lesbian and gay speakers bureau in the San Francisco public schools, objects to White stereotypes about Latin machismo. As an example, she recalls a school administrator who "carried himself gracefully and spoke in a polite manner." One of Chris's White colleagues said meaningfully, "I told you he wasn't married." But Chris has another explanation.

> By this particular Latino administrator's behavior, another Latino or Latina would not assume that this man is gay, because a Latino gentleman is expected to carry himself with dignity, gracefully, and cultivate both his masculine and feminine aspect. But to Westerners [Americans], that kind of softness is associated with gay men. . . . We lay on all these assumptions. . . . A lot of homophobia is really part of the way the Westerners have divided up the world.

Phil Robinson believes that racism is at the heart of White assumptions about rampant homophobia in communities of color.

> It's always a question why we have to have a litmus test . . . of who's more homophobic than others. Like, to make the African American community homophobic, does that mean that the White community isn't? Or does that mean the Asian community isn't, or does that mean the Latino community isn't?

As they define and redefine their relationships with their home communities, lesbian and gay teachers of color feel a special bond with their minority students. Doralynn started a support group for the Black children in her school, a residential school for the Deaf where many of the students are children of color but most of the teachers are White.

> The racism against the kids . . . was really painful to see. . . . These are kids that come from . . . a home where their family is Black, their community, their neighbors, their friends, their church—and they are pulled out of this safe, familiar place and moved to a predominantly White environment where they have to sleep and eat food that's unfamiliar and [be around] people that don't know how to comb their hair. I mean these are little kids and they just freak out.

Doralynn's example inspired a Latina teacher to start a Hispanic–Latina/Latino support group the following year, "which is great," Doralynn says, "because there's a lot more of them and they have the same kind of difficult experiences."

Alan Miller, one of three Black teachers in the twenty-member English department at California's Berkeley High School, goes out of his way to volunteer for departmental projects, especially the grading of student proficiency exams.

> I do it because it's important that there be a Black person involved in the workings of the department. You know, it would look very strange if all the people who graded the proficiency exams, which determine who graduates from the school, it would be very strange if all those people were White.

Sometimes teachers of color are disappointed by the communities they hoped to serve. Daniel Cevallos, a Colorado music teacher, took a job at an inner-city middle school "in a very low income Latino neighborhood," hoping that his presence would inspire his students to "help themselves. . . .

There are lots of avenues and lots of resources out there available to them if they would just reach out." But Dan has grown frustrated.

> They were not reaching out, even though I made all this apparent to them, and it was almost as if they didn't want to. They liked the way they were and they wanted to stay that way. . . . I could not take these groups out into the public anywhere without fear of them throwing gang signs and getting in trouble.

After four years at the school, Dan has reluctantly decided to look for another job in "a more affluent neighborhood, and actually a more White neighborhood." The move saddens him, for Dan's Latino culture is very important to him, and he has been upset at the racism in the gay White movement.

Joseph speaks enthusiastically about student teaching at a school where half the students were children of color. "That's the kind of school that I feel more comfortable in, 'cause the students look like me, and I look like the students," he says. "There're so many minority kids out there that aren't aware of what their potential is yet, and if they can see that maybe Mr. Martinez is doing it, you know, maybe they can do it too."

But not all teachers of color subscribe to the "role model" theory of self-esteem. Phil Robinson agrees with the sentiments of Black novelist Toni Morrison, who asks, "Why is it that it's only in the African American community that we always feel that having a role model will shore up the race? Why don't they say that about other races as well?" For Phil, acting as a role model means caring about all his students' lives and sharing all the parts of his identity with them.

Like gay teachers of color, members of other religious and cultural minorities feel a kinship with their minority students. Nancy teaches her Deaf students that Deafness is not a disability but a culture, with its own customs and its own language, American Sign Language. Her desire to nurture their self-esteem grew out of her experience teaching at a Deaf school in the south, where she was required to abandon ASL in favor of Signed English. Unlike ASL, which is a visual language with its own syntax, Signed English attempts to reproduce spoken and written English in signs, in a process resembling transliteration. "It's not even a sign language, it's a code," Nancy explains. "They forced me to take Signed English classes every week. . . . They would correct me. They would tell me my signs were wrong."

Lesbian and gay teachers who have known economic hardship say that the experience of poverty can can also be an inspiration to care for students. Jean Bourg, who was one of six children growing up poor in a "Cajun-Catholic" family in Louisiana, is especially outspoken in her defense of students who are "different"—"alternative-type kids," both straight and gay. Pam says her childhood in "a large family, fairly poor," affected the way she relates to her students at a large working-class high school in Central Maine. "I think that type of struggle allows you to be more empathetic. . . . Education and self-esteem [are] things that kids don't have enough of. . . . They don't see good role models, so they put themselves down," she says.

Many minority teachers speak of racism in the gay community, which they see as a reflection of attitudes in White society as a whole. Jill Beppu and Pat Soon belong to APIHEP, the Asian Pacific Islander Homophobia Education Project, a group of Asian American gays and lesbians who speak to audiences in Seattle's Asian community. Both are frustrated at the racism they encounter in the White gay world. Pat, a social worker and former high school chemistry teacher, criticizes the overt racism in the mainstream gay community. "When you go to a lot of gay bars if it's a really busy night they'll card Asian people but they won't card White people," he says. "It gets to the point where I get so frustrated by it I just don't go there."

Pat's work as an advocate for disadvantaged youth and adults has made him aware of prejudice against disabled people within the gay community.

> I deal with a lot of clients who tell me that they're gay. I think it's difficult for people with disabilities in general, especially with mental disabilities. . . . Within the gay culture, the perfect gay person is White, flawless, and male. That's where the power seems to be.

Jill, an artist and art educator, is dismayed by the internalized racism she finds within the Asian gay community. She wonders why Asian lesbians and gays are content to identify with the pink triangle, the symbol worn by homosexuals in European concentration camps and now used as a symbol of gay pride by the mainstream gay community. Jill would like to see her community create its own symbols, "something for Asian Pacific Islanders."

Dan Cevallos is discouraged to find himself the only Latino at many gay events, like the Denver teachers group whose meetings he attended several times. There, Dan says, he "felt like the token representative of the Latino community—again."

Other lesbian and gay teachers of color say that they, too, have felt like "a token." Torey was barely out of his Harvard graduate teaching program when a suburban Chicago high school flew him out for an interview and hired him on the spot. His first class at the new school was a summer school history course, where the mostly African American students complained that the school was not meeting their needs, that the teachers were racist and the administrators indifferent. He told himself that the students were probably bitter about having to attend summer school. But once classes started in the fall, Torey became increasingly suspicious about why the school had been so eager to hire him.

> There was a Hispanic American teacher in the history department who . . . was raising such a big stink that the news about his problems had reached me in Boston. . . . He was fired. He wasn't asked to return. . . . He was a good teacher and he had all these students supporting him.

Another conflict involved a student who had been forbidden to wear a kilt, "part of his parents' Scottish heritage," to his prom the previous year. Torey wondered, "If this outfit is considered formal attire in the Scottish community, why is he not allowed to wear it?" Administrators avoided his questions.

> All they were telling me was that . . . as an African American you're needed. And I later came to find out more and more as the school year went on, that, oh, yes, I'm definitely needed as an African American at that school but not necessarily because . . . I am a capable teacher.

Eventually, Torey discovered that the school had been accused of racism by the local Black community. "They wanted to do their part to appease the local NAACP by saying, 'We've recruited this African American man from Harvard. He's going to be part of the history department.'" Torey was so disillusioned that he decided to leave after his first year.

Struggling to cope with racism, anti-Semitism, and other prejudices in the mainstream community, and with homophobia in their home communities, many gay teachers find parallels between the different kinds of oppression they experience. Jewish lesbians and gay men, for example, point out that both these identities can be invisible in mainstream society. Sometimes they even talk about "coming out" as Jews in the same way that they talk about coming out as lesbian or gay. Susan Mayne, a middle school teacher in suburban Connecticut, explains:

> I'm Jewish and I went to school and was raised in an almost all Jewish school. I now teach, work, live in a really WASP-y environment. . . . [Those] parts of me are invisible. So in that sense they're kind of the same, and I feel really awkward making a point of either one.

Michelle teaches at a West Coast school for the Deaf where the student population is far from "WASP-y"; students come from ethnically diverse backgrounds, and the school itself espouses the "bilingual-bicultural" philosophy that promotes Deaf culture and ASL. Yet as a Jewish lesbian, Michelle still feels invisible.

> We had "Secret Santa" week, and I kept getting all these Christmas-y gifts, even though I told the person that I was Jewish. She wasn't even realizing that they symbolized Christmas. . . . We had a holiday party and I raised my hand at the staff meeting and said, "Instead of a Christmas party, can it be called a holiday party?" And they said, "Fine," and then I was told to go buy the napkins and plates and I was asked to buy all red and green.

Michelle goes on to suggest the peculiar way that people who are "different" can feel uncomfortably obvious at the same time they feel invisible.

> You can count on one hand the Jews on campus. And everyone knows who they are, which shows you what a minority we are. If everyone knows who the lesbians are and everyone knows who the Jews are, you can tell that there aren't that many.

Gay and lesbian educators of mixed heritage have an even more complicated task. Pat Soon explains:

> My mother was Korean and the Korean culture tends to really be Christian, but my father is Chinese and Chinese tend to be Buddhist, so . . . I grew up within this Buddho-Christian culture. Within the Asian culture, of course, you just cannot be gay, because the Asian culture is so focused on longevity of the family and having kids and grandkids. . . . It was really hard putting all this together.

Doralynn grew up thinking she was White, until an uncle visited with his five children, who "were darker than I was and had frizzier hair than I did." Her father, who is darker-skinned than her mother, has a Seminole, French, Spanish Creole, and Central American heritage; her mother, who "is very light-skinned and passed for White all her life," had a French grandfather. Meeting her Black relatives precipitated a major crisis in Doralynn's life.

> I had to go through this whole transformation . . . besides being a preteen, teenager, figuring out identity in a general sense, sexual identity, racial identity, all of that stuff was very confusing.

Doralynn now identifies herself as a Black lesbian, though she adds, "On any given day it may be a different answer, because being mixed race has its own list of things." But she feels that "doing all this work on me [has] made me stronger to be out there." It has also made her a fierce advocate for her Black and mixed-race students.

Alejandra Dubove's family came to the United States from Argentina when she was two years old. She now teaches at Chapel Hill–Chauncey Hall, an independent school in the Boston area, where she has come out to her students and staff. Alejandra compares her coming out as a lesbian to her coming out as a Latina, for both have involved struggles with denial, privilege, and oppression.

> Our parents drove into our heads that we were Argentine, and that we weren't like the rest of South America, we're this elite group of people. So when I moved to Texas, having these ideas in my mind, and seeing how people who were Mexican were treated in Texas—which is horrendous—I didn't want to identify with being Latin, so that people wouldn't call me Mexican. . . . When I moved up here [to Massachusetts] I didn't find much of a Latin community, so I never really thought of myself as being different. . . . In the last few years I started thinking more about what it means to be Latin, and why I didn't want to identify with that, because I didn't want to be discriminated against. . . . Kind of like the same way I dealt with my gay identity. I didn't want to be labeled as a gay person, I wanted to pass as straight.

Alejandra's desire to embrace both identities has led to what she calls "a renaissance" in her life.

> It's been a time of change for me, a kind of a time of self-pride. I'm Latina and a lesbian, and I want that to come out, I want it to shine, I want to understand more of what these identities mean.

Some gay teachers suggest that different parts of their identity have been important at different stages of their lives. Chris Rodriguez, now thirty-one, says his "primary identification" is "around . . . ethnicity and color," but admits that "at eighteen I felt very different. . . . At eighteen I was clearly more identified around my sexual orientation than I was anything else."

Phil Robinson, who is a poet as well as an educator, acknowledges that when he first came out, the writers who meant the most to him were Zora Neale Hurston, James Baldwin, and Langston Hughes—all gay and all African American. "At that time," Phil says, "that was me, that was my development, that's what was missing." Now, at forty-four, he identifies with "the community that I live in, which is a community of many ethnicities and cultures. That is the community that I'm out to."

Like their Black, Asian, Latino, and Native American colleagues, White teachers who work in communities of color are also forced to consider the meaning of race in their lives as gay educators. Teaching in ethnic communities different from their own, they make inevitable comparisons between the attitudes of White and non-White students. Cary says that his Hispanic elementary school students are not afraid to show affection.

> When they leave my classroom I always say, "You can either shake my hand or give me a hug," and generally, even the older Hispanic boys hug me. . . . Now the parents probably would have a real problem with it.

"Joel," a White high school teacher of English as a Second Language, has had a very different experience teaching Hispanic students in the Mission district of San Francisco. During one field trip to the San Francisco Zoo, a Chinese boy and an Indian boy, both about seventeen, began holding hands as they walked along. "The Latinos went nuts. They were like, 'You can't do that. They're gonna throw stones at you. That's wrong. That's bad. That's awful.'" The self-conscious students stopped holding hands, and Joel "was really pissed off . . . at the fact that these Latinos were so closed-minded and so schooled in homophobia and machismo."

In his frustration, Joel blames machismo without considering whether a group of White teenagers would have behaved the same way. Part of his anger stems from his vulnerability as a gay man, and his inability to respond to the Latino students as he would have liked.

> I didn't say to them like, "Shut the fuck up," or "You know, you're full of shit," or "Let them do what they want to do," which of course my gut feeling was. . . . If I had done that, it would have put me in a position of terrible vulnerability and they wouldn't take me seriously, and I couldn't teach them.

Eventually Joel decided to address the subject of machismo through a class discussion. "I cut out this article I found in the local Spanish weekly about machismo and the world of men, and I thought, okay, this is good, this is how we learn, and I can be objective and just let them have it out."

As the students discussed the article, the conversation turned to the subject of gays in the military.

> There was a range of opinion. Some people used pejorative terms referring to gays. . . . Some thought that it was okay, because gays are human, and I was kind of impressed by that. Other people . . . were toying with the fact that homosexuality in itself was wrong and they had moral objections to it. And as we continued to have this discussion about gays in the military and

machismo, I was totally unprepared when one of the students asked me point blank, "Are you heterosexual?"

Joel says he was afraid to respond because of the "cultural differences" between him and his students. He says, "They're coming from one of the most homophobic cultures on the planet, Mexico. I mean they have gay murders now . . . and that makes me very reluctant to respond to them." At the same time, he realizes that his students' difficult behavior reflects their dislocation as immigrants:

> A lot of these kids leave Central America and they come here from Mexico without their parents. . . . They feel totally uprooted. They deal with poverty and language problems . . . and racism, I'm sure.

Other White teachers who have been targeted by students of color share Joel's mixture of frustration and sympathy. Annette has endured blatantly homophobic attacks from African American students at her inner-city high school. At times, she feels as though the Black students are incapable of identifying with anyone else's oppression.

> This African American woman tried to show this video that she taped from the Oprah show on gay teens and their school in New York . . . and so she told the class what she was gonna do and they started chanting that she was a faggot lover. . . . She finally just turned off the video and said, "Well, you know we can't do this today." This is a straight, African American teacher—a wonderful human being and a wonderful teacher and she could not control or conduct a discussion [on] how discrimination makes these people feel and how it hurts.

But Annette also realizes that the Black students' behavior is symptomatic of larger issues—racism, sexuality, and oppression. "There's a lot of anger, these kids have been abused . . . there's a lot more hopelessness too. For them it's a land mine or something."

David Bruton, a White teacher who endured threats of violence after he came out at Chapel Hill High School in North Carolina, thinks the Black boys in his school are the most homophobic members of the population.

> The most incredible kinds of comments come from the Black boys. Every now and then a Black girl will say something that indicates she really just doesn't think this is the way it ought to be, but she's not nearly as critical as the boys are. . . . The White boys are not quite as outspoken as the Black boys are. There's a good deal more of laughing and joking that the Black kids engage in, while the White boys tend to define their responses along

the lines of, "Well, you know, I just don't think I'd feel very comfortable in the shower, showering next to a gay boy."

But not all White teachers think their students of color are especially homophobic. Lyn Boudreau, who taught for a year in an inner-city junior high school, does not recall having "any more trouble with the Black kids than I did with anybody else." Lyn remembers a playground incident in which both her accuser and her defender were Black:

A couple Black kids were eighth graders who really didn't like me because I disciplined them. . . . One kid came up to me and said, "Hey, is it true you're a lesbian, man? We've heard about that." And this big Black girl said, "Oh, don't you be givin' her a hassle. Don't you be hassling her." He just stood back. And it was okay, 'cause she was kind of the mama.

Pat Tomaso recalls many confrontations with both White and Black students during her years as a playground supervisor for the Chicago public schools. She feels that the real issue is honesty and trust.

I would sit down with the kid and try to explain the situation. "My job is to keep you, your brothers and sisters, and all these other children on this playground safe. What you're doing doesn't allow me to do that because you're not playing in a safe way, or you being here with your gang members attracts other gang members to my playground and they're gonna be firing at you, but they're gonna miss you and they're gonna hit somebody else." . . . Whether you're a lesbian or a straight person, they respect you because they know where you are with them and what's what. At that age, that's what they need more than anything else.

Some White gay teachers say that students who have known oppression are more likely to empathize with lesbians and gays. Tim Brown says the mostly Latino students in his high school lesbian and gay support group "see the parallels" between racism and homophobia. "Their experience with racism helps them when they try to counter homophobia," Tim says.

"Rina," a White elementary school teacher who spent seventeen years teaching in Harlem in the 1960s, felt completely at home among her Latino students and their families. "It was very family-oriented," she recalls. "The parents were very wonderful. . . . I had a lot of godchildren. A lot of the Latino parents wanted me at their children's birth."

Rina was explicitly out to her principal and her colleagues, and was even tacitly out to some of the parents. "I had a lot of gay friends at work. . . . We all stuck together, and at a school where there's so much oppression among the people, the staff becomes very cohesive. . . . I did not feel any kind of homophobia."

Leslie's inner-city high school is about 80 percent Latino, and she says her experience has taught her that the White image of the macho, homophobic Latin student is "very simplistic and condescending."

> I see some of that traditional crap and I want to kick people in the butt, but I see girls challenging it as well and I've seen girls in a mixed class of thirty-five to forty kids take on some of those boys about sexual orientation. "What is your problem with this? What? You can't deal with it?" I love it.

Leslie's relationship with her Latino students extends beyond the classroom. She and her partner have lived in the neighborhood where she teaches for over fifteen years.

> I'll tell you what I see among these Mexican American kids. I see few of these families throwing their [gay] kids out. I think that there is more, you know, "I'm not happy with what you are, but you are my child." . . . They're part of a unit and much more so than what I see Anglos do. I've come to really respect that.

As they discuss the complicated issues of race and class, gay educators applaud efforts to promote diversity within their schools. Many have joined these efforts. At the same time, they resent the fact that lesbians and gays remain invisible even as schools acknowledge racism and sexism. They point out that gay culture is still missing from new "multicultural" curricula, and that many administrators who have established policies against racist name-calling still tolerate homophobic slurs. "Tom," a hearing high school teacher at a Midwestern school for the Deaf, says that he reported a student who called another student "nigger" during an assembly, but decided not to write up a student in his classroom who called someone "faggot." He explains, "I thought my principal wouldn't back it up. She would go through with consequences if it was 'nigger,' but not 'faggot.'"

The exclusion of gay culture from the "diversity" umbrella breeds resentment between White gay teachers and teachers of color and creates competition among people who should be one another's allies. Susan Mayne was sitting in the lunchroom at her middle school when another teacher started describing a trip to Provincetown, Massachusetts, and explaining how she had to "protect her kids from all these homosexuals." Susan was so upset that she left the room, almost in tears.

In telling this story, Susan identifies the teacher as Puerto Rican, though the woman's ethnicity seems irrelevant to the rest of the anecdote. Asked why she happened to describe her colleague this way, she answers, "I'm just thinking of her. She's a very dynamic, chatty, colorful kind of person and makes terrific rice and chicken that she brings in to school." But a moment later, Susan touches on something deeper.

> She was involved in all our diversity workshops. We were trying . . . to put together a high school diversity week and the powers that be decided that gay issues weren't going to be a part of this, because we only had a week and therefore there were other things that were more important. So it became just cultural, the Latino and African American. She was part of that and she has a Puerto Rican exchange over here. And so part of my—I guess anger is that she's visible. . . . People can learn about Latin culture and music, but it's not okay to learn about homosexuals.

Susan's final words show that she understands the way institutionalized homophobia divides White gay teachers from straight teachers of color. Her anger at the Puerto Rican teacher has nothing to do with prejudice against Puerto Ricans, and is only partly related to the woman's remark about Provincetown. The deeper hurt comes from the way Susan's school has ignored her culture and denied the reality of her oppression.

White teachers are not the only ones who resent the exclusion of gay issues from school diversity initiatives. As part of her advocacy for students of color, Doralynn has insisted that her administration sponsor diversity inservices for the staff. The workshops have been a good start in raising awareness about race and culture, but the school is still not dealing with homophobia.

> People are saying okay, I need to recognize Blacks are someone, you know, and these Mexicans can do something other than eat beans. . . . They'll say, okay, I will acknowledge something. But there is no room in the world for gays and lesbians.

Listening to gay and lesbian teachers of all cultures and colors, it is clear that the process of defining an identity is complicated and complex. What is equally clear is that homophobia does not exist in a vacuum, but is connected to racism, sexism, and all the other oppressions that make people invisible. Creating safer schools for gay teachers and students means building alliances with educators from other targeted groups. Yet therein lies the unique paradox of gay oppression. Reaching out to a straight ally means becoming visible as a lesbian or gay teacher. And while lesbian and gay educators know that hiding is what keeps homophobia in place, for most of them it is still a way of life.

PART TWO

Hiding

I can't reach out
To the ones who need a friend
I must pretend to be
One of the enemy . . .

Ron Romanovsky, *"One of the Enemy"*

4

Being Invisible

IN A GROUND-BREAKING STUDY FIRST PUBLISHED IN 1992, University of Massachusetts Professor Pat Griffin described the "identity management strategies" of a group of lesbian and gay educators.[1] "Passing," the most closeted strategy, involved presenting oneself as heterosexual and lying, if necessary, in order to do so. "Covering" meant that gay teachers censored their words and actions but did not explicitly lie. "Implicitly out" teachers assumed others knew of their sexual orientation but did not declare it publicly, and those who were "explicitly out" were able to name themselves to the school community as lesbian or gay.

When teachers talk about passing, covering, and being implicitly or explicitly out, they suggest many subtle variations of these strategies, along with other methods they use to make themselves feel more secure. D. J. Reed, who is mostly out in her Seattle-area high school, says that many gay teachers try "to be way above our colleagues in terms of how we deal with kids on a professional level, the quality of what we do." She adds, "I think a lot of gay teachers are so good because their fear is if they're average it's not good enough."

Jeff, who is out to a few of his parochial school colleagues, agrees: "You kind of overcompensate sometimes. Like, you have to be the absolute best, perfect model of a teacher all the time. You just end up driven."

---

[1] Pat Griffin, "From Hiding Out to Coming Out: Empowering Lesbian and Gay Educators," in *Coming Out of the Classroom Closet*, ed. Karen Harbeck (New York: Haworth Press, 1992), pp. 167–96.

Many others feel they need to be outstanding in order to be seen as equal to their heterosexual colleagues. "If there is anything I do to compensate, it is that I work very hard," says Jean Bourg. "It never hurts. . . . Model teacher. Model lesbian. Model free thinker. Model happy person. That's all I can do." Claire says she preserves her security as an elementary school counselor by being "really careful to build my base of support with my parents and my staff."

Being implicitly or explicitly out, instead of passing or covering, does not remove the pressure to be a model teacher; if anything, educators whose colleagues know they are gay feel even more pressure. Kevin Gogin, who coordinates support services for lesbian and gay youth in the San Francisco Unified School District, works in a relatively gay-friendly environment, and his employer is a city agency rather than a school. Still, Kevin admits, "I have the tendency to anticipate any problems that may come along and be as squeaky clean as I can possibly be, so that then there is no room for discussion."

As part of this preoccupation with their professional image, gay teachers think a great deal about their appearance, not because they are particularly vain, but because they worry about being identified as lesbian or gay. Gay male teachers may monitor their gestures and speech, while lesbians often talk about clothes and grooming. Jean Bourg describes her school clothes as as "camouflage: I dress like a teacher. I wear jumpers, blouses, and skirts."

For many lesbians, "dressing straight" is a painful reminder that they are not free to be themselves in the classroom. Gwen, who worked in industry before becoming a middle school science teacher, feels "self-conscious" about her appearance in school.

> As a geologist I could wear khakis and kind of be androgynous looking and it wouldn't be a big deal, but for school I needed to be something a little bit more. I started to mess around with hairdos and for the first time in my life this stuff was really having meaning to me and I thought, "This is ridiculous."

Nancy Goldstein eventually left her job as a school social worker because the strain of "trying to pass as straight" was too intense.

> It was horrible. . . . I would dress a certain way, maybe so I would look less butch-y . . . like little girl shoes and, you know, wear a blazer and dress pants. I wouldn't dress how I'd feel comfortable or the way I dress up myself when I go out.

Lesbians who choose not to conform to straight dress codes feel just as uncomfortable. Fran Gardner, who has left her elementary school teaching job, says her appearance was part of what isolated her from her straight colleagues.

> They were all married and they were all very quiet and they all didn't speak out politically, and they all shaved their legs and blew-dry their hair and wore makeup every day. . . . I wore my hair . . . shorter, freer, wilder. I don't ever wear makeup. I don't shave my legs and I don't do anything to disguise that. . . . I wore Birkenstocks.

Grooming and attire that contradict traditional female standards often provoke harassment from straight colleagues. When Ruth cut her hair shortly after the beginning of the school year, the principal at her Georgia elementary school kept telling her she should let it grow long again because it looked "real pretty" that way. "The last time he said it, I said, 'Yes, and my ex-husband liked it long too.'"

For lesbians who do not look stereotypically butch, the opportunity to pass brings protection, but it also brings inner conflict. "Christy" finds that her straight appearance allows her to conceal her identity in her work with special needs children and their parents.

> I wear makeup, I wear dresses, and I don't look like your typical right lesbian, and matter of fact a lot of lesbians say, "Well, I didn't know you were a lesbian," as if I was supposed to have a crew cut or something.

But being taken for straight sometimes makes her feel guilty.

> It feels safe sometimes to pass. . . . But I'm always having to make a choice to come out as opposed to saying, "Well, I'm out, because look at me." . . . I am not comfortable about that, because it feels like I'm buying into the whole notion of homophobia.

Laurie, another lesbian who is often taken for straight, agrees that "being able to move in and out of worlds" is a mixed blessing. "I work it to my benefit, but sometimes it doesn't work because people don't know what to make of me."

Protecting a gay or lesbian identity from disclosure extends beyond clothing to other aspects of a teacher's appearance. Symbols like "freedom rings," rainbow stickers, or pink triangles are a source of pride to many gay and lesbian people, yet most teachers do not feel comfortable displaying them at school. With symbols, as with everything else, there are degrees of safety and disclosure. Few teachers would consider wearing a "freedom ring" neck-lace or a pink triangle pin in the classroom; some might have one on a coat or a backpack. Stickers on cars carry a slightly reduced risk, since they are not brought into the classroom, but they are still visible to students and staff walking through the teachers parking lot. Tom bought a rainbow sticker one summer and put it on the window of his car; by fall, he was debating: "Should I take this off before I go back to school?"

Along with monitoring their appearance and censoring their behavior, most gay teachers are constantly aware of what they say and to whom. At one end of the spectrum, teachers who are completely closeted at school remain silent about their personal lives, or, if questioned, construct an imaginary het-erosexual existence complete with opposite-sex partner or spouse. They are willing to lie about themselves if necessary, in order to preserve their safety. Linda, who is now tacitly out at her coastal Maine high school, was very care-ful "not to be identified" in her first teaching job. "I talked about my boy-friend in Boston and I had a picture of a friend of mine in my wallet. I had a copy on my desk."

Teachers who present themselves as heterosexual are often uneasy about the moral implications of lying. Lisa, a Massachusetts elementary school teacher, felt a strange kinship with a student who told her that his father was in jail, and begged her not to tell anybody else. "Now he's got this big deep dark secret. It's like, 'Well, kid, so do I. I've got a dark secret too. I've got to be hush about mine, you be hush about yours.'"

Some teachers justify lying as a matter of self-protection. Dan Cevallos says he would be willing to lie in order to keep his job.

> If I had to admit that I was gay and I was to lose my job as a result, I would deny it. And I wouldn't be denying it to me. I would just be saying, "Hey, you know, I need a job. I need to eat." And if I need to tell these people a lie to save my job, I will.

Hiding a gay identity means altering facts about one's life, changing the names of places and people in order to appear straight. The most common example is the "Monday-morning pronoun," in which gay teachers change the gender of a partner during casual conversations with colleagues. Laurie resorted to this strategy after a breakup with her girlfriend.

> It came to a point where I had to talk about it. I was changing pronouns. . . . It became such a complicated way of dealing with it because I'd have to remember what I said and how I said it and what I was talking about. I had to really pay attention to my own self because I had to calculate.

Fran Gardner describes some other pronoun strategies she used as a closeted elementary school teacher.

> I talked a lot about "we." "We did this." "We did that." . . . When everybody else is talking about their husband and their spouse . . . you say, "A friend and I did this, a friend and I did that, we did this," with never a name, with never a gender. . . . Someone said something once about "your boyfriend," and I went "What?"—not being able to correct it and say, "No, no, no, my girlfriend."

Changing pronouns, or using "gender-neutral" language, is more than just a grammatical exercise. For teachers in significant relationships, concealing a partner's identity means denying the existence of the most important person in their lives. It means listening to humiliating remarks by straight teachers, who are usually unaware of the effect their assumptions have on lesbian and gay colleagues. Sue's description of a faculty-room conversation is a good example.

> We have our staff get-together coming up . . . and it's you know, bring your spouses. And I thought, "Okay, well, that lets me out." And then the person who's organizing it said, "Yeah, bring your spouses but there's no children and we're all a bunch of old married people anyway." . . . I was actually pretty mad. I was sitting there and I just kind of dropped my head and I didn't say anything because being first year in the building I don't want to cause any kind of a stir at this point.

Sometimes teachers decide to bring their same-sex partners to school events, either because they think the staff environment is safe enough to do so, or because they finally get fed up with hiding. Jan Goodman, who is now out as the principal of Jefferson Elementary School in Berkeley, California, says that in her first job as a principal she "avoided social events like the plague" for two years, but finally changed her mind.

> Well, I'm gonna go to the stupid administrator thing and I'm taking my lover. . . . I went around and I practiced, "This is Sheila, she's my p-p-p-." Am I gonna say "partner"? Am I gonna say "lover"? Am I gonna say "life partner"? What am I gonna say? "This is my spouse"? So I finally just said, "This is Sheila, the woman that I live with," or a couple of times I said, "partner." I couldn't say "lover."

Ruth and her partner have been together for a number years and have even had a commitment ceremony. Ruth recalls the time when they met as one of the happiest in her life, yet it was also a time when she felt the pain of hiding most strongly.

> After I met her my head was just flying. . . . This one teacher that was real real straight, she was just like, "Hey, hey, who is he?'" And we have this machine that has food in it, it has "Tom's" [crackers], and I just looked over there and I said, "Tom," and so she kept egging me on about "How's Tom doing?" . . . After a couple of months, I just couldn't stand the fact that I had this lie going around inside of my head. I just said, "We're not together any more."

Michelle met her partner just before she moved to the West Coast to begin her first teaching job. All that year, she endured the ups and downs of a commuting relationship while remaining in the closet at school. Hiding was especially painful after a long visit from her partner.

> It was very early in the morning and it wasn't until I was driving to work in my car that it suddenly hit me that she was gone and I wouldn't see her for a long time. I started crying on the way to work. It was just really sad, feeling all lost and missing her and wishing she was still here. And then I arrived at school and I parked in the parking lot and I had to completely clean myself up, straighten myself up and act like nothing was wrong. I was still wiping my face, blowing my nose, and then a coworker pulled up next to me in the parking lot and as I got out of the car I had to act like nothing whatsoever was wrong. . . . I was afraid that if she noticed something was wrong that I would start crying again.

Leslie and her partner "Margaret" have been together since "Emily," Margaret's biological daughter, was an infant. "I have most of my social pain around not being able to say, 'Yes, I'm a parent,' to anyone," Leslie says. "I could say, 'This is my stepdaughter.' 'Oh, are you married, Miss Lane?' 'No.' 'Were you married?' . . . There is no name for me."

Leslie also resents the way her relationship with Margaret remains invisible to her colleagues, while heterosexual marriages are freely celebrated.

> One guy got married last year. It was a second marriage, and they had a very small, go-to-the-justice-of-the-peace sort of thing, but we put money together and bought him a gift and a card, and I didn't say, "Well, you know, Margaret and I never really had a ceremony."

Closeted gay teachers miss the support of their colleagues in hard times as well as in good ones. A heterosexual divorce, however messy, is likely to elicit the sympathy of the teacher down the hall; a lesbian or gay breakup must be hidden from colleagues who do not know that the "ex" was a same-sex partner. Chris, an Iowa junior high school teacher, remembers the isolation he felt when he and his partner broke up.

> My lover of eight years left last April. If somebody was going through a divorce at school . . . everybody would know . . . and people would be supportive. . . . Here I was just trying to survive through the end of the school year, it's like terrible, and yet I couldn't tell anybody what was going on.

Though gay teachers agree that passing is painful and humiliating, the identity management strategy with the greatest potential for stress is what Pat Griffin calls covering—trying to avoid disclosing a gay identity without telling an outright lie.

"I won't lie about the fact that I'm gay, but I won't be totally honest about it either," declares Bill, who is especially careful because of his position as an elementary school principal. "I've had students say to me that their uncle saw me in a gay bar on Saturday night and . . . I just kind of glossed it over and changed the subject in a hurry."

"Bert," a teacher at an independent school in Ohio, wishes he could be more open about his life but remains "somewhere in the middle" between lying and disclosing. "When people talk about their weekends, I don't make up stories. I just don't say anything. That's not good but it's better."

Gary, another teacher who conceals his identity without actually lying, remembers the one time in his life when he did have to lie about being gay.

> When I was drafted and filled out the little form, they still had the question on there—*the* question. I checked "No." . . . And I've never denied it since. . . . But I don't remember another time where I had to say, "No, I am not." . . . I'm smart enough to do all sorts of other things.

Concealing a gay identity can be especially stressful in job interviews, where truth telling has legal as well as moral implications. Lisa recalls a student-teaching seminar where a professor discussed how to answer personal questions during interviewers. "It pushed a real panic button. . . . It's very tricky not to lie but to just not offer information." Thomas Juul, who is relatively out as a middle and high school audiovisual director, finds that applying for administrative jobs has pushed him back into the closet, especially when the subject turns to his research on the lives of gay teachers. "During an interview I had someone ask me about my dissertation, and it kills me but I modify it. . . . I go off on this tangent."

Laurie, who, like Tom, is a teacher-turned-graduate-student, says she began censoring her research as soon as she thought about sharing it with others.

> Originally, I wanted to do more with gay/lesbian students and homophobia, and when I was just sitting by myself or in my class or writing papers, that was a real safe thought and a very empowering thought. . . . But then, thinking about coming to these places and presenting, or people asking me about what it is I'm doing, made me a lot more cautious and a lot more scared.

Covering is especially difficult when students start asking personal questions. Many gay teachers, like Ron, plot their answers in advance.

> One of the students said to me point-blank . . . "Rumor has it that you're a homosexual. Is that correct?" . . . I had been kind of anticipating that that might come from one of the students so I sort of rehearsed it beforehand. . . . I said, "To be quite frank with you, my sexuality is none of your business. . . . It's none of your business for several reasons. One is, it's inappropriate for you to be asking me this in front of a group of students. If it's something you want to talk about privately, I could talk with you about it privately. . . . Number two, I don't know you that well, and it would be totally inappropriate for me to be talking intimately about myself." . . . Of course that didn't quash the issue. It continues to be an issue.

Others try to deflect or avoid the question, especially when it is asked indirectly. During his first year as a high school teacher, rumors began to circulate about Dave Larson's sexual orientation.

> Some of the students were wondering about this rumor, and they wanted to check it out, and one of them asked me, "So, what do you think of Cindy Crawford?" And I said, "Well, you know, she's not really my type, but my friends met her." And I'm trying to tell the story of how my friends in Comedy Sports had met Cindy Crawford, and then it was like, "Oh, that's really cool," and then they forgot the reason that they asked me in the first place.

Cary, who is slightly more open with his students, answers the question without actually saying that he is gay.

I just say, "Are you sure you want to know the answer? . . . Because I'm gonna tell you the truth." And generally the people who have asked me say, "Well, I guess you just told me the truth, didn't you?" "Yep."

Often, these encounters with students can be frightening. Shirley was walking through the parking lot outside her high school when she reprimanded a group of boys who were smoking.

I said, "Hey, guys this isn't the smoking area, you know, you can't smoke out here." . . . And one of the boys behind me says, "Are you straight?" He didn't say it really loud, but I could tell it was directed at me, but I was already past him so I just pretended I didn't hear it . . . and then he said it again, "Are you straight?" He didn't yell or anything, it was just he asked me twice, but he was behind me so we weren't making eye contact. I mean, if we were actually having a conversation I'd have to deal with it.

Sometimes a question comes as a comment meant to be overheard. Deann was returning from the tennis courts after a high school P. E. class when she heard two girls behind her talking very loudly.

One said to the other, "Well, you know, Ms. LeBeau's a lesbian." I just turned around and I said to them, "So what if I am. What difference does it make? Would it make this class any different?" And they just sort of looked at me. "No, I guess not." So I didn't affirm it, but I didn't deny it, either.

Dianne describes a similar experience that took place in the hallway of her junior high school, when she heard a girl behind her say loudly to a friend, "Do you know she's a lezzie?"

So I thought, I have a choice right now, I either ignore it or deal with it. I told my kids to go back to my classroom, which they did, and I went to the group, ferreted out two kids that could have been possibles. Mean-spirited children that would do that kind of thing to anybody, whether it was "nigger," or whatever. I took them to the office and told the principal and he dealt with it. That kind of thing, it doesn't happen frequently but when it does happen it just rips at me.

Like Dianne, "Keith" discovered that confronting student harassment was an effective strategy. He was walking into the main building of his Colorado Springs high school one morning when someone in the parking lot yelled "faggot" five separate times.

I decided I would not give him the satisfaction of confronting him in front of other students. So I went into the school and I found out the name of the [student]. . . . And then I went to the assistant principal and I said, "I want this student brought in and I will be down here to meet with him in the morning."

Keith brought a tape recorder to the meeting, and told the student he was taping the entire conversation.

He wanted to know why, and I said, "Because if I decide to take legal action, I want this on tape, and I also want your parents to know what you say." . . . Of course he denied it at first, and then when he knew he couldn't deny it he said, "Well, I'm gonna call my mother." I said, "Please, call her. We need to get on with this." Well then he didn't call his mother. . . . The assistant principal made him write me an apology and bring it to me. And he and I actually got along quite well after that.

Often, students ask their gay teachers if they are married, or have any children, or have a girlfriend or boyfriend. Since this question is also asked of straight teachers, it is sometimes difficult to know the exact intent. (An unmarried heterosexual teacher who is frequently questioned by her male students says, "They want to find out where you are because they're so paranoid about where they are.")

For gay teachers, questions about their marital status are frightening as well as uncomfortable. Such questions carry the threat of disclosure and make teachers wonder if students are asking out of sheer curiosity or because they suspect their teacher is gay. Lynn responds to questions about her personal life by saying, "I have too many kids. I don't have time for my own. No, I'm not married." Barb sometimes tells her middle school students, "'I never met a man I fell in love with'—which is the truth." Bob Bradley says that in the years before he was out to his junior high school students, he would answer their questions with humor. "I said, 'Why should I be married? I don't like kids.'"

Curt recalls a conversation with a high school student in which he decided to reveal his identity without actually saying he was gay.

We were coming from an event and she was sitting in the front seat of the van, and the rest of the kids were in the back, the music going, talking or something . . . and she said, "Mr. Lawrence, are you married?" And I said, "No." . . . She said, "Oh, I thought you were." And I said, "No, Annie, I'm not." I said, "I'm forty-five years old and not married, a male." And I looked her straight in the eye and I said, "Think about it, Annie." And she looked at me real funny and then said, "Oh, well, that's okay."

Though they may feel compelled to lie, evade, or censor their responses to students, most gay teachers wish they could be more open. Like Michael, they find that "being invisible is what hurts us and helps us; it's our friend and it's our enemy." Hope would love to show the middle school students she works with "that it's okay to be gay, you don't have to end up a certain way, you can be very successful, and attractive, and dress nicely, and, you know, be in good relationships."

Dan Cevallos likes to imagine what his students might say if they learned about his sexual orientation after leaving school. "Wow, you know, he didn't act gay, he didn't look gay, but yet still he is and he was a great teacher and, well, maybe being gay is okay."

Jan Goodman, who remained mostly closeted in her first job as an elementary school principal, used to imagine a similar scenario.

> I had fantasies years after I left that *20/20* would come and interview me and they'd go back to my old school, or *Sixty Minutes* or something, and they'd say, "Did you know Ms. Goodman was a lesbian?" And the kids would say "No," but they'd say all these really nice things, and how it didn't matter.

Meanwhile, most gay teachers walk the line between concealment and disclosure, never knowing exactly how much their colleagues and students actually guess, and never sure exactly how they would react to the truth. Michael explains:

> It's like you're always one decision away from disaster. That's what you feel like. You feel like, one person getting this information, the wrong person, could destroy my life. . . . It's one thing for people to think I'm gay, but for them to have that confirmation, there is a difference.

Wondering how much others know, or guess, can create a kind of cognitive dissonance for a lesbian or gay teacher. Lynn says that although she is out in most of her life, she is never quite sure how she appears to the parents of the special needs children she works with. "I don't go around with an *L* on my chest or anything but I wouldn't say that I am really closeted. I have a hard time picturing how I am."

Alejandra Dubove, who is now explicitly out to her students at Chapel Hill–Chauncey Hall in Massachusetts, remembers how anxious she felt when the headmaster took her aside shortly before the beginning of her first year and asked her if she knew about a court case involving a lesbian teacher. (The teacher, Chris Huff, had been told that she would have to live in campus housing, but could not live there with her partner. Her case was defeated and is currently under appeal.) Alejandra had never heard of Chris Huff or her lawsuit, but her first reaction was anxiety.

> I'm thinking, Why is he saying this to me? Is it because he knows I'm a lesbian, is it because he's trying just to be up front with me, is there a hidden meaning, or is he just giving me information?

Such uncertainty can make even an experienced teacher feel insecure. Bill says he frequently does "a little reality check with my friends, saying, 'Do you think this is too out?'" But for a new teacher, faced with all the usual worries about how students will respond, the anxiety is even greater. Joseph recalls:

> When I was doing my science methods course we had to videotape ourselves. I saw myself on tape and I was like, wow, do I really act that feminine in the classroom? . . . I wish I didn't act so feminine. . . . In my teaching, I'm always thinking, well, don't swing your arms too much, or whatever.

All this uncertainty and insecurity isolates gay teachers from their colleagues and students. As a school psychologist in Marin County, California, Allan Gold often works with students' families.

> I get invited to Seders . . . and Bar and Bat Mitzvahs, and—should I bring somebody? So I pretty much self-identify as, you know, single, asexual. . . . I'll talk about other teachers' husbands or other teachers' children. It's like I don't have this life outside school other than, you know, people know about my Victorian house, and people know I like to travel, and people know I like to cook or paint or, you know, those facts about myself—as if I have no other life.

Jan Goodman describes her life as a closeted administrator as "principal by day, lesbian by night." She says:

> I spoke at classes for the Gay and Lesbian Speakers Bureau. I would say I was a principal. I never said exactly where I was a principal. I was writing articles about gay issues and the lives never crossed because I had to be myself somewhere.

Shirley, who has become more closeted since the passage of Colorado's antigay Amendment Two, says hiding keeps her "from being the teacher I used to be. You know, building the rapport. There's always that wall, you know, that would stop you [from getting] too close."

Most painful of all is the way hiding keeps gay and lesbian teachers from building relationships with their colleagues. Judi, an elementary school teacher in rural Maine, says:

> I feel locked out. I've always felt like I haven't ever really had a close buddy, and when I talk to other teaching friends, how important that is, to have a real good buddy. And I don't know whether I push myself away from everyone. It's probably a combination of pushing myself away and me imagining that they're not accepting me. So I always feel a step away from pretty much everyone I teach with.

Rina experienced the same isolation when she moved from the Harlem school where she had been fairly open to staff and administration to a new position in Queens, where she felt she needed to conceal her sexual orientation. The job itself was "spectacular, teaching-wise." Rina's excellent reputation had followed her to her new school: parents wanted their children in her class, and her kindergartners loved her.

> But when I got into the teachers lunchroom, all of a sudden I couldn't be who I was, and that was new to me. So I didn't go. I didn't because I was afraid they would start asking me questions. Then I figured, I want to go. I mean, I can't isolate myself because it's not good professionally to isolate yourself, because the staff can really do you in if they don't have a grip on who you are. . . . So I would go into the teachers lunchroom maybe three times a week.

Self-protection takes a great deal of work. It takes planning. Above all, it takes energy that could be focused on teaching and learning. As Jeff says, "I'd just like not to have to waste my time constantly kind of thinking."

But the energy teachers spend on hiding is more than a drain on their time; it is a drain on their minds and bodies as well. Chris is convinced that if he didn't need to hide, "my anal sphincter would relax another two inches." Linda remembers her closeted years as an emotional nightmare.

> My whole construct was to completely lie at school. I just felt so on the brink and I was under so much stress. I was so miserable. I felt so crazy. I couldn't imagine being honest with anybody there.

Michael measures the strain of being closeted at school by comparing it with two years he took off from teaching.

> It was wonderful. I joined about ten different gay groups and I never once had to worry about, is there a student, do any of these people know any

student, do these people have any relationship to the school I'm teaching in, is there any way that this can link to the school. It was like being out of prison for two years. And now I feel like I'm back in prison.

Ron explains the difference in terms of greater vulnerability.

I know there's homophobia out there in other jobs and occupations too, but being an educator I think you're particularly vulnerable because you're dealing with students, you're dealing with parents, you're dealing with the community, and you're very much in the spotlight.

This combination of repression and fear can lead to an array of physical symptoms. Karen developed an ulcer during a confrontation with a group of parents who tried to get her fired.

I got a bleeding ulcer last fall, I thought, "This is crazy." I nearly quit my job, because I thought, "It isn't worth dying over, this is not worth ruining my health." . . . There are times when I think to myself, God, are you just some sort of masochist?

Even Dave Larson, who talks confidently about how comfortable he feels as a gay teacher, has experienced his share of physical symptoms.

I had . . . my third date ever. . . . I got to school on Monday morning . . . and before school started I had this panic attack that somehow everyone knew and it was all over. . . . There were a couple of days after that, where I had this sense that the whole world was rushing in on me every once in a while. . . . There were some days it was intense, and some days there were none. . . . You know, like shaking before school and it only lasted about ten or fifteen minutes in the bathroom, and I got through the day.

Peggy admits that having to pretend has affected her health.

Among other things, I weigh forty pounds more than I did when I got involved with [her first same-sex partner]. I don't drink, I don't do lots of other damaging things to myself, but obviously food has become a problem to me. Part of the reason I went into therapy was that I had this sense that I'd weigh three hundred and fifty pounds if I didn't.

Rina suggests that the stress of hiding was at least partly responsible for her breakup with her former partner, also a teacher.

She was new to the gay world, had a difficult time with it, and stories started to fly about her. . . . I didn't say anything. I never said a word. I kept it hidden. I was getting agitated. . . . I'm not gonna blame it all on her. We were both becoming homophobic.

Rebecca remembers the strain of teaching as a closeted lesbian in Wyoming.

I'm surprised I didn't get an ulcer living back there. . . . The coping strategy I had was getting in the car at three o'clock on Friday when school was out and driving five hours to Denver to get away. To find any kind of gay community support. Not being from there, you didn't build a network, you just went. To the gay bookstore, to the bar, to the gay disco—and then, on Sunday you drove back knowing that on Monday it would start all over.

Rodney stayed in a heterosexual marriage for years after coming out, partly to protect his teaching job at the Christian school where his daughter was a student.

There was a bookstore on the other side of town from where I lived and the school is and all the families in the school live. . . . It was a two-story old house and the downstairs was a bookstore and the upstairs was all the little booths, where men get together. . . . I would fall asleep on the couch, or pretend to, my wife would go to bed, and I would get up at twelve o'clock and stay out 'til two or three in the morning. . . . And she never knew.

Doyle Forister, who is completely out at Skyview High School in Billings, Montana, remembers a gay teacher whose emotional distress ended in tragedy.

I had a real good friend in Great Falls. . . . He said, "You told your folks? I never could tell my folks." . . . End result: about a year and a half later [there was] an accusation against this man. . . . The school district said, "We have reports that your truck has been parked behind a gay bar and you can either resign or we will have a public hearing into this." And he hooked a garden hose onto his exhaust and asphyxiated himself outside of town. . . . I have never forgiven the society that took Mike's life.

Given the burden of hiding, it is not surprising that many lesbians and gay men leave teaching, or wish they could. "I'm thinking of possibly getting out of education altogether," admits Ron. "Part of the reason is the homophobia. . . . I just get worn down after a while. I'm just sick of this shit, don't want to do it any more." "Wendy," who is completely closeted at her elementary school, feels "frustrated with the entire system. It's not that I don't love children and I don't love giving them the gift of learning, it's just that I'm tired of not being treated like a professional, like an adult. I'm extremely burned out and I've only been teaching three years."

Two teachers who have left the public schools, Nancy Goldstein and Pat Tomaso, have found it easier to be gay in the outside world. Nancy quit her school social work position after four years, and says that she will never return to education. "It would make me sick physically," she declares. "It would be a step backward to do that, because, you know, the goal for me is just to be authentic in my life, and that means being a lesbian." Pat elected an early retirement plan from her job as a Chicago public-school playground supervisor, and feels as though she has been "let out of the cage." She says:

> That was the only place where I wasn't out to any faculty or anybody. . . . I started to beat myself up for not being brave enough to do it while I was working, but I realized that every person has to do what they need to do.

But for the teachers who remain, hiding is a constant strain. It prevents them from forming authentic relationships, from turning to colleagues in moments of joy or distress, from feeling that they are truly known for the people they are. Most of all, it renders them invisible. Deann LeBeau speaks for all those who are still hiding, as she remembers her feelings during a presentation on homophobia. She was sitting in the back of the library when the guest presenter told a group of fifty or sixty students that there were gay and lesbian people all around them, and probably in their own lives as well.

> One of the things she said was . . . "Now, raise your hand if you know someone that's gay or lesbian." And maybe five or six kids raised their hand. And I was in the back of the room, and I wanted to say, "What about me? What about me?"

5

One of the Enemy

MOST GAY TEACHERS KNOW THE NATIONAL STATISTICS THAT reveal that lesbian and gay adolescents are at greatly increased risk of suicide. They hear the daily name-calling and gay-baiting that echo through the halls of most American schools; they see physical attacks on gay students go unpunished. While any teacher with a conscience would be troubled by these injustices, gay teachers feel something more. For them, the shouted epithets and the quiet desperation recall their own adolescence, and stir them to want to make things better for the gay youth in their schools. As Jeff puts it, "When you get called a faggot or something like that in high school—I don't think anybody has any sense of what that feels like."

Gay teachers long to show their students that gay adults can lead happy, productive lives. They realize that unlike students in racial or religious minorities, gay youth have no community of people like themselves to return to at the end of the day; indeed, they may go through their entire adolescence with no image of themselves other than the negative ones projected by mainstream American culture. Pam speaks for many of her gay colleagues when she describes her feelings about the gay students at her high school.

> That's the toughest struggle, to see kids and not be able to reach out to them and say, "Yes, I do know what you're going through.". . . In my whole process of coming out . . . I didn't identify myself as a lesbian or being gay at all. If I put a label on it then I had to assume all the negative stereotypes that had been given to me, and it took me a long time to sort out the difference.

Christopher Rodriguez, who works with lesbian and gay youth at the Harvey Milk School, is appalled by their isolation.

It's disturbing to see just how little support exists for these young people, particularly in a place like New York where you imagine there is all kinds of innovation and progressive organizing. . . . They've never known other young people like themselves, never known an adult in their lives who was gay or lesbian identified or who was supportive or receptive to someone who identified that way.

Gay teachers are especially distressed when gay students are harassed, beaten, or driven out of school. Pam recalls a series of incidents involving three teenage boys at her school who all came out at about the same time.

The majority of it [was] verbal. There [was] a little pushing, shoving kind of stuff. There was one fight . . . where the kid was being harassed, but they both got punished the same, which is typical. . . . One of them went to the principal and said, "This is going on and I'm being harassed and pushed around." . . . The principal actually said to him, "Conform and that won't happen. Change your dress." . . . And so with that kind of support the kid said, "Forget this. This is not safe for me to be here." . . . And so he dropped out. . . . The other two kids that were his friends . . . one went to another school and was harassed there so he just dropped out, and those two kids to my knowledge haven't been back.

Sometimes, lesbian or gay teachers even acquiesce in the unjust treatment of gay students because of their own fears of being exposed. Tracy Phariss, a Denver middle school teacher, describes one such teacher at a school near his.

A student was chased out of the high school with three baseball bats. . . . The parents were real supportive. . . . They were worried for his life. They had no support from the public school system. . . . I talked to a lesbian teacher, and she said, "Well, he was just so flamboyant about everything." . . . She is a totally closeted lesbian teacher telling a student who is openly gay that he deserves to be [assaulted] because he's here rattling the system.

Some have experienced the gay teen suicide epidemic firsthand. Two years ago, a pair of girls in Hope's school district took their lives by jumping onto the train tracks of the Long Island Railroad.

The first thing I said when I heard that they had done it together, was, they were in a relationship. And everybody thought I was crazy. Sure enough, they found their journals and as it turned out they were bisexual and they were involved in a relationship.

As a result of the tragedy, Hope felt compelled to become more visible to the gay and lesbian students at her junior high school.

> I put a sign on my door about what to do if a friend tells you they're gay. I had so many kids coming into my office asking me questions. . . . I thought, if those girls had somebody that they could have talked to, would it have been different?

"Mary" keeps several gay-themed books on the "Teen Topics" shelf in the media center where she works as a school librarian. Several years ago, a young man checked out *When Someone You Know Is Gay* along with a book on suicide, explaining that the books were for "a friend." Later that spring, the boy tried to kill himself.

> I lost touch with him because it was the week before graduation. I wrote him a note but never got a response. I think his parents were guarding him and praying for him to change. I've heard since then [that] he was in the hospital because of the attempt, but [he said] if he got out he'd try again.

Such stories make gay teachers want to show their lesbian and gay students that being gay need not be a cause for despair, or, as Terry Minton says, "for a kid growing up in this little town not to think that the only queers in the world are the ones that they see singled out in the Gay Pride parade on the news." But giving this reassurance would mean coming out to students, and such a risk seems impossible for many gay teachers. Dianne says:

> I would like to feel safe enough to have the kids know from me that, Yes, I'm a lesbian. This is my life and it's not just a "sexual life-style" but my life. Because I know pretty well that some of them are going through the same things, fears, anguish, all the stuff that you go though. I want to be able to be a support for those kids, but I don't feel safe enough. I want to be seen as Dianne Wilson, language arts teacher, not Dianne Wilson, queer language arts teacher. And that's what it would mean if I told them.

Joseph knows that when he leaves college for his first teaching job he will be in the classroom "not only as Hispanic but as a gay individual." But because of his insecurity, he feels "more comfortable with the Hispanic side of it. . . . The gay side of it I wouldn't even touch in the classroom." Nevertheless, Joseph plans to keep his classroom safe for gay students by not allowing homophobic remarks.

> 'Cause as time goes by . . . and as more people come out, a lot of the students that we see are gonna have family members that come out, and

they're gonna have moms or dads that come out. . . . Even though it's gonna be awkward, they're gonna feel a little more comfortable with it.

When he left the Christian school where he had taught for so many years, Rodney doubted that he would ever return to education. But he says that the desire to help gay youth might make him reconsider.

I think maybe the only thing that might make me go back is if I felt like I could really do something good as far as being openly gay . . . and being a role model and guiding kids through those difficult, difficult years, especially if they were like I was and don't know anybody that's gay. They could avoid a lot of the heartache I had and a lot of the heartache I caused other people by . . . finding someone to love the way their body tells them that they are to love.

Some gay educators have become convinced that the best way to help gay students is to work for policies that allow lesbian and gay teachers to be out in their schools. Ron and Barb led the struggle to add sexual orientation to teachers' contracts in Portland, Oregon. They were initially inspired at a 1992 conference where they heard a keynote address by Virginia Uribe, founder of the Los Angeles youth support group Project Ten.

"I guess the thing she said that kind of got us going is that there's no whole hell of a lot you can do for students unless the teachers are protected," Ron says. Barb adds:

You know, this is all fine to be able to start providing these services for gay and lesbian kids, this is what the conference was about, for them, but where we don't have any rights in our contract for sexual orientation and when we're scared to death to be who we are, we can't be very helpful [to] them.

Donovan Walling is a former junior high school teacher and central office administrator who now edits special publications for Phi Delta Kappa, the national education honorary. In recent years, he has compiled several handbooks on the needs of lesbian and gay teachers and students. Looking back on his years in the classroom, he agrees with Ron and Barb that protection for teachers is a prerequisite for affirming lesbian and gay youth.

Until teachers feel comfortable being openly gay, they're not going to be out there to help students. Students that I saw struggling—I wasn't open enough that they could even think of turning to me. It wasn't something that would have occurred to them.

Bert worries about the lesbian and gay youth at his Ohio prep school, and wishes he could reassure them.

> I would like to retire in six or seven years, and I can't afford not to keep this job, so there's that on one side. The other side of me is thinking of all those kids, kids who are becoming gay and lesbian who might benefit greatly from a model, and also all the other kids, the 90 percent who might not end up quite as homophobic if they saw that some kind of normal, regular everyday people happen to be gay and lesbian.

Leslie feels the same frustration, which she shares with another lesbian teacher at her high school.

> Both of us are family people. We both have stable lives, we're both healthy individuals, we're both doing what we love. . . . And we both have incredible guilt . . . over the role models that we could be if we had the courage.

For gay teachers who cannot step out of the closet, every encounter with a gay or questioning student seems like a missed opportunity. David Bruton recalls an incident that took place before he came out at his high school. A student in his class had been called "faggot" by another student, and although David had reprimanded the offender, he still felt uneasy. He asked the student who had been insulted to stay after class.

> I told him I was just flat out at a loss to know what to do in a situation like that without making it worse for him or for the class, whatever. And he said, "Oh, don't worry about it. You know, that didn't bother me." Just tossing it off, it's no big deal. And of course at the time I was convinced that it was a big deal and he was trying to convince me that it wasn't. But there was nothing else that I could do. And that has sort of haunted me all that time since then.

Such encounters can be incredibly complicated affairs, in which both teacher and student dance around the real issue without ever feeling free to name it. Rebecca remembers one exchange which left her, too, feeling "haunted."

> A boy . . . came bopping into my room between classes, came over to my desk. The class was empty and the kids were getting ready to come in and he says, "Miss Harris, are you gay?" Very blunt question. I looked at him and my heart sank and I had a million and two thoughts going around in my mind. Am I honest with this kid? I don't know this kid. Is he trying to out me? Could I lose my job? What's going to happen if I tell him the truth?

What do I do? Is he gay? Is he asking me for support? Does he need help? All these questions went through my head. The kids started to come back into the classroom and I said, "No." . . . Maybe he really needed my help. He's not back at the school this year. I don't know what happened to him. But that haunts me to this day.

Not surprising, Rebecca's first response was fear for her own safety ("Is he trying to out me? Could I lose my job?") Yet side by side with her personal anxiety was her desire to care for the student ("Is he gay? Is he asking me for support? Does he need help?") What "haunts" her is not only the knowledge that she was unable to be "honest with this kid," but the thought that he might have needed her help.

Sometimes, gay teachers are able to help gay and questioning students without actually coming out to them. One of Annette's high school students came out in a classroom essay.

I just encouraged her. I said, "Oh, that's great, you know where you are and you can accept who you are," and talked about family support and stuff. But I would have liked to come out to her. She knew I was gay but I didn't want to acknowledge it. . . . There're just so many barriers.

Fran Gardner, who now works as a children's book buyer for a small bookshop in Massachusetts, and Mary, the high school librarian, both try to provide gay youth with relevant reading material. Fran is careful to put gay magazines "out there where the kids can see them," and stocks the bookstore with titles like *Young, Gay and Proud*. "We've lost a few copies," she admits, but says she is glad that "if kids are gonna steal something, at least they're stealing that." Mary reports that gay titles are likely to disappear from the shelves of the school library.

Annie on My Mind has disappeared so I've replaced it probably three times. . . . All of the others, I notice some of them are not on the shelves now and they don't always get checked out. They don't always go through the checkout process.

Anne says that as a middle school counselor she can usually identify the lesbian students, and goes out of her way to include them in her support groups.

I'll usually try to be their counselor just because I want to be there and support them. . . . In the group it will come up about the boys and girlfriends and things—I will usually bring up some of my own stuff, like when I was a kid, I really preferred playing sports and doing these things and I never wore a skirt until I was in seventh grade.

Hope provides the same reassurance to students in the groups she runs as a junior high school social worker.

We talk about maybe not necessarily labeling themselves at this point. That at fifteen years old you can have a wide range of sexual experiences. One boy in particular thought he might be gay, and he was thinking of making this statement to everybody, and I just told him about the consequences of what might happen, how not to label himself right now. I never push them either toward or away. I always talk about the feelings.

Lesbians and gay men sometimes joke about "gaydar"—the sixth sense that seems to enable them to recognize one another without any obvious clues. Whatever the nature of this power, it apparently begins early, for gay students seem to find their gay teachers no matter how discreetly closeted the teachers think they are. Nancy Goldstein recalls that during her four years as a school social worker, "word got out to the gay kids and I was like a magnet." Deann LeBeau says that several of her high school students have come out to her after leaving school. "I've found after they've graduated it seems to be more comfortable for them. I have lots of little friends now that I had as students."

Nancy is only partially out at her school for the Deaf, but when a counselor approached her to ask if she would talk to a senior boy who thought he might be gay, she agreed.

I said, "You know, he's Deaf and he needs a Deaf role model as a gay person." . . . Now he comes up to me often and we communicate and we talk about it. And he says, "You're a lesbian, wow." . . . I told him, "You better not tell your friends, though, in the high school, because you know, they haven't been exposed to my teaching."

Teachers who are relatively open about their lesbian or gay identity are even more likely to attract gay students. When Carolyn Wood moved to a new job after seven years of closeted teaching, she came out at school for the first time.

The [first] seven years that I taught I didn't see a gay student in my classes. Then I came out and that one year I saw every single one. It was like a shade went up.

Thom Juul was approached by a gay student when he came to school wearing a souvenir T-shirt the day after the 1993 March on Washington.

> I had never seen him before. Big guy. He comes over to me and says something about the T-shirt. And it took me a second. I said, "Oh, yeah," and he just gave me a look and a couple of sentences that said he knew he was gay. Here he was, a macho football player. . . . I'd seen him with girls and the whole routine, but he was announcing to me that he was gay—the fact that he knew there was somebody else in the building.

Occasionally gay teachers are surprised to find that life has actually gotten better for gay students since the days when they were teenagers. D. J. Reed, who coaches softball at her high school, marvels at the self-possession of the young lesbians on her team.

> At fifteen, sixteen, seventeen, [they] are very comfortable being lesbians and they talk about it and they love it and they think it's really cool. And I'm like, "You guys, life's harder than that." . . . I advise them to do some reading, to call these phone numbers, to go to some support groups.

Being sought after by gay students is not without its perils. Even an openly gay teacher like Carolyn Wood feels uncomfortable when she suspects that a student's problems go beyond sexual orientation.

> This one who I know . . . wants something and I just don't want to be involved in that. It's like I get a nervous feeling. I can feel my hair on the back of my neck change. She came in the room a couple of times alone and I just thought, this is trouble, this is big trouble.

Carolyn isn't quite sure why she has a strange feeling about this particular student, but she fears a scenario in which the girl "does something damaging to herself and writes about it in relation to our class or something. . . . Or her parents read things that she's written and then say I was encouraging her to do that."

Hope has been harassed by an eighth-grade girl who she suspects has a crush on her.

> She started making crank phone calls to my home. Somehow she got my home phone number. And a couple of her friends had come down a couple of months ago, saying that this girl said that she was gay and they didn't know what to do about it. And of course the girl denies ever saying something like that.

Gay teachers realize that this unwanted attention often arises out of desperation. They know from bitter experience how lonely a gay teenager can feel, and most try to steer their gay students toward support groups and appropriate reading material. Some decide that only by being completely open can they provide the kind of support their gay students need and deserve. "Lynne" is a high school teacher who came out to some of her students during her second year of teaching. At the end of that year, her junior/senior English class was studying the Holocaust.

> I decided for their final project they would each pick a group of people that's discriminated against and study that group.... We had a brainstorming session, and they yelled out all different groups, and one kid said, "gays and lesbians," so I put that up there. At the end of the brainstorming session I said, "I want you to think about which group you want to study, and tomorrow you'll let me know which group you want."

One of the students in the class was a boy whom Lynne had referred to counseling earlier that year, and who she suspected might be gay. When she handed out the list of groups the following day, he pointed to "gays and lesbians" and said that was what he wanted to research.

> I was so thrilled, because he was in the back of my mind the entire time I designed this project.... I felt what this kid really needed is a place to start exploring gay and lesbian issues.

As part of the project the boy wanted to interview a gay person. Since he didn't know anyone, Lynne introduced him to a man who had worked in her school the previous year.

> He called and set up the interview, and he went and ended up staying there until ten-thirty at night, asking questions for hours. He wrote in his report that it was the first time that he ever met a gay or lesbian person.... Several weeks later, after thinking about it, I said to him, "I read your report, and you said in there that you never met a gay or lesbian person. But you've met me." ... And he said, "I know, but in the outside world." And it made me really glad to think that he knows about me. 'Cause I drop lots of hints, but you think you're dropping really strong hints, and people don't get it.

Part of the requirement for the final report was for each student to do an oral presentation.

> He got up to present his, and he was swaying so much that the kids said, "Stand still." ... When he planted his feet, he knees were shaking so much

you could see it right through his pants, his legs were shaking like twigs. But he presented his whole report and . . . the kids were fine.

On the same day that the student gave his report, another student, a boy in Lynne's freshman class, sought her out after school.

This kid, who I had had very strong suspicions about . . . looked at me and said, "So, another student told me that you're chaperoning at the gay prom. I want to go." I was flabbergasted. His directness and his sincerity were so different from any interaction I'd had with him all year, it was like he was a different person. And then he proceeded to ask me all kinds of questions. He asked me when I knew I was a lesbian. He asked me if I felt that people accepted me. I felt it was really important how I answered that question. He was obviously wondering if he was going to be rejected in life or not. So I stressed the importance of finding allies and finding a community and other people who are like you . . . and that of course there's discrimination, but it's a lot easier when you find a community, and that there's a community out there.

Lynne took the freshman boy to a meeting of the local gay youth group and helped him arrange to go the the gay prom. She is glad to be able to help her gay students feel good about themselves. But she acknowledges that mentoring them brings its own set of risks. When she dropped the boy off after the youth group meeting, she says, she hoped "that no one was seeing this and getting the wrong idea." She also thinks "it would probably feel very different and feel very much riskier if these were female students."

Lynne plans to continue reaching out to her gay students, especially those with no other supportive adults in their lives. But she knows she must draw some boundaries in her work with them.

I think I tend to get maybe on the edge and a little too fanatical about it, because I just get so worried knowing the suicide rate for gay teens, knowing the statistics. I have to be careful that I'm not responsible for saving all these kids. I can get rather obsessive, and there have been kids I haven't been able to get off my mind for days because I'm worried about them going back to their families.

Although he is not openly gay as an elementary school teacher, Rick has begun working with school counselors who run programs for gay teens.

I let them know that I am a gay educator and that I have some concerns about how gay teens are treated and harassed in the high schools, and that if there's a teen who needs more than just a school counselor, I'm not a trained counselor but I am a teacher, and that I could listen to them.

Reaching out more openly in this way "has been kind of scary," but has enabled Rick to help a number of young gays and lesbians cope with their own coming-out issues.

I've taken 'em out to Wendy's or somewhere and just talked, and . . . a couple of 'em have cried a little bit, really scared to tell their parents, scared to let their friends know. . . . I guess I wish I would have known earlier in my life.

Leslie decided to take the risk of coming out to a girl in her class who disclosed her sexual orientation in a personal essay.

She said things that really frightened me, like, you know, "I feel like I'm always gonna be alone, I don't feel like there's anybody I can talk to, I don't feel like life is worth living, I can't tell my mother, I can't tell my father."

That night, Leslie discussed the essay with her partner Margaret and their daughter Emily. Both urged her to come out to the student.

She told me when I came out to her that she suspected that I might be [gay]. . . . I told her that I had read her essay and I thought she had a lot of courage and that I really respected that. . . . I directed her toward Outright and toward some other groups and let her know that there were a lot of other kids and gave her some leads, some titles to some books. . . . She would come and visit me and then she took two classes from me in the second semester.

Gay teachers who are willing to disclose their identity may also be able to support children in gay families. When a girl in Michelle Serries' middle school class asked if she was gay, Michelle had to choose between safety and disclosure.

In order not to get in trouble, I said to her, "Well, it's difficult for me to answer that question because I have been told that I'm not supposed to." And this girl looked at me and she said . . . "You should be proud of that. My mother's gay." And so then I explained to her, "Yes, I am gay, but there are adults that are troubled by that and don't want me to share that, and I am trying to stay out of trouble."

The girl was so excited that she brought her mother and her mother's girlfriend to the next parents night.

She said, "Mom, Mom, this is my gay teacher." And her mother turns around and she goes, "Don't say that. You know, it might get her in trouble." And I said, "No, no. We've already talked about this."

A few teachers have gone beyond coming out to one or two gay students and have become advocates for gay youth on a wider scale. Several years ago, Timothy Brown came out to a gay student at his high school. Soon, word got around. Tim talked with other students, and "gave them a book or two." Soon, he went to an administrator, asking for permission to form a student support group. A gay psychologist volunteered his time and helped Tim draw up a permission form for a "health issues" group at which students might discuss a host of topics, including pregnancy, suicide, smoking, and peer pressure, along with sexuality. The form allowed students to participate with parental permission, without explicitly labeling the group as "gay." The group now meets regularly in Tim's room, and includes anywhere from five to fifteen students. Tim says he originally hoped "just to target some kids because I wanted them to feel supported," but he is now tacitly out to the staff and students. He even wears his "freedom rings" to school—"although not very often."

Kevin Gogin works as an advocate for gay youth in the San Francisco Unified School District, where, despite his city's reputation for openness, he finds that not everyone feels free to come out. Many teachers still recall the climate created by the 1978 Briggs Initiative, which would have mandated the firing of all California's gay teachers.

A lot of the teachers [are] afraid that if they come out they'll lose their job. Not right now, but maybe some day. Or they just remember the fear of it, you know, running rampant.

Gay students, too, are more closeted than one might expect in the nation's gay mecca. "Most of the kids I talk to would no more come out to their classmate than they would, you know, fly to the moon," Kevin says. Through his work with teachers and students, Kevin is able to help young gay people work through their fear and denial, and to develop a positive identity. He remembers one Asian student, a senior when Kevin first met him.

They were . . . new to this area. The mother was completely distraught. . . . The son said, "Well, I can't possibly be gay . . . because I want to be a doctor." . . . And then he kind of progressed to a point where he could come out more and more and more.

Just over the bridge from San Francisco is Berkeley High School, a multiethnic, heterogeneous institution where twenty-seven hundred students attend grades nine through twelve. The students are Black, White, Latino, and

Asian, with a substantial immigrant population. Many are biracial. A glance at the *Jacket*, Berkeley High's weekly student newspaper, shows that the school has celebrated everything from Asian Pride to Cinco de Mayo with assemblies, guest speakers, and curriculum workshops. Yet according to Alan Miller, who has been teaching there for four years as an openly gay man, Berkeley High is still woefully deficient in meeting the needs of its lesbian and gay students. As a case in point, Alan describes an incident in which members of Project Ten, Berkeley's gay, lesbian, and bisexual support group, were booed and jeered when they spoke at the 1994 International Women's Day assembly.

In an article published in that week's *Jacket*, Alan and a lesbian teacher criticized the administration for allowing the harassment to continue. The principal defended his failure to intervene by saying that "students don't respond to being talked at." His inaction angers Alan, who says that despite the presence of a half dozen openly gay teachers and the existence of Project Ten, Berkeley High School still has a long way to go in making its lesbian and gay students feel safe.

> I was told about a colleague—this was a Black colleague—justifying the behavior because "the assembly forced lesbianism down their throats." . . . He defended what happened in his class, in which people made very, very homophobic comments which he allowed to go unchallenged. He said that he wants them to say what they feel. Fine. But would he as a Black man allow racist comments to go unchecked? I bet he would not. The kids would not leave the room with the impression that it was okay to make those kinds of comments.

This incident clearly shows that no matter how multiethnic a school or how multicultural its mission, gay and lesbian students will continue to be harassed unless advocacy for them is explicitly included in the diversity agenda. It also shows that all the support groups and diversity initiatives in the world are ineffective without strong administrative leadership.

Most gay teachers live and work as a small minority within their schools, and struggle to convince administrators to pay attention to the needs of gay youth. But Christopher Rodriguez spends his working life mentoring lesbian and gay students at the Harvey Milk School, one of only two schools in the United States devoted exclusively to sexual minority youth.

The Harvey Milk School was founded in 1985 as part of the Hetrick-Martin Institute (originally called the Institute for the Protection of Lesbian and Gay Youth), a nonprofit social service and advocacy organization established in 1979 by A. Damien Martin, an NYU communications professor, and his partner Emery S. Hetrick, a psychiatrist. Hetrick-Martin now serves over seven thousand young people a year with counseling services, a drop-in center, and the Harvey Milk School, an alternative high school that operates under the auspices of the New York City Board of Education. The school has two full-time teachers, along with a paraprofessional teacher's aide. In addition, many adults volunteer to teach a class or lead a workshop.

The thirty students who attend Harvey Milk are referred by social workers or counselors, or sometimes by family members or through word of mouth. Because the school exists to serve students with no other support system in their lives, most have been victims of gay-bashing or abuse. Fully 75 percent are dropouts from other schools. But Chris Rodriguez prefers to call them "survivors."

> Many of these young people don't have very good communication skills by virtue of their experience in the public schools. Many don't have very good negotiating skills by virtue of the experiences they've had in their communities at home and in school. So that's really the foundation for the work. We have to teach and model good skills so that these young people can be better advocates on their own behalf and so that they an get these credits that they need to graduate.

Chris says that the volunteers who work at the school do not need to be gay or lesbian, just "good role models [with] strong teaching skills and very good boundaries." But he also thinks that gay youth need positive gay adults in their lives.

> It's very, very important for young gay, lesbian, bisexual, and transgender people to have role models, not only out in the world, like media figures, but also in their daily lives . . . people that they can look up to and ask questions to and interact with. . . . It's really a big opportunity for them. So we try to make the most of it.

Few teachers work in an environment where they can be as openly supportive of gay youth as Chris Rodriguez and the teachers at the Harvey Milk School. But most do what they can for the lesbian and gay students in their schools. Whether they are running a support group, or slipping a copy of One Teenager in Ten onto the library shelves, or just giving a gay student an extra-friendly hello in the morning, gay teachers are making their schools a little safer for students who might otherwise have no allies at all.

PART THREE

Horror Stories

"I can hear him saying to me, 'I think the world stinks and I think people are awful, but for the good of the school, I have no choice but to not renew your contract.'"

Bert, *high school teacher, Ohio*

6

Another Kind of Fear

MOST TEACHERS WHO HAVE BEEN AROUND FOR A WHILE CAN remember the fears that kept them awake before their first days in the classroom. Will I be able manage a room full of ninth graders? What if students ask me a question and I don't know the answer? How will I find the time to plan my lessons?

Gay teachers, especially inexperienced ones, share these universal worries. Like all new teachers, they find reassurance in the advice of experienced colleagues, and in the expectation that confidence will come with time. But gay teachers know another kind of fear, one that cannot be dispelled by experience or good advice. The fears that haunt them have nothing to do with their ability to teach. They come from forces outside their control—from the hate, lies, and suspicion that create a hostile climate in classrooms and schools.

Underlying all these fears is the one great fear of losing the opportunity to teach. Gay teachers know that in most places they can be fired outright because of their sexual orientation, or they can be harassed, humiliated, or pressured to resign by parents, students, or others in the community. For those who consider teaching to be their primary identity, the thought of never being able to teach again is devastating.

Most gay educators are conscientious teachers and administrators, liked and respected by students, staff, and parents. Yet when they talk about their fears, it is clear that few of them feel really safe. Jan Goodman was popular and well respected during her years as a closeted elementary school principal. But she admits she was always planning for the worst. "I had to be twice as good, because I was amassing this record that I would then bring to the

Supreme Court after I got fired," she explains. Ruth has an excellent relationship with the administration at her elementary school, yet she fantasizes about being called into the principal's office without warning. "[He] sits me down, says, 'I hate to inform you of this but you have been terminated because we do not want an image of homosexuality at this school.'"

The fears can begin even before a gay teacher is hired. Dave Larson recalls his interview as a nerve-wracking experience.

> Just in general, job interviews wreck your self-esteem because you think, "They're looking for a reason not to pick me and I can think of one really clear one right now." ... The one thing I worried [about] most ... was not, am I a good teacher, or can I handle students, or do I have ideas about how math should be taught in school, but it was, what will they do if they find out I'm gay? Will that keep them from hiring me?

The most worrisome part of hiring and firing decisions, as many teachers point out, is that it is not always easy to know whether a decision has been based on a teacher's sexual orientation. Pam declares, "Say what you want to say, if you're going to be fired for some reason, there's no way to identify the real reason."

Before she was hired at her Oregon elementary school, Karen Cosper applied for a position that was offered and then abruptly withdrawn. She says, "I'll never know what happened but I'll always have this little thing in my mind—did they find out? Did they talk to somebody? ... You just never know."

Karen's school system guarantees that teachers cannot be fired because of their sexual orientation. But she points out that even with such contract language, "a lot of things can happen." Lisa and Mary teach in Massachusetts, where workplace discrimination based on sexual orientation is against state law, yet both express fears similar to Karen's. Lisa points out:

> You have to have money to afford to go to court. There are lots of organizations that could come in and help, but then the time and energy—and then you become this political—"Oh, yeah, I remember her, she's the one who rocked all those boats over in that other town." You get blackballed, I'm sure, if you make waves.

Mary says the state law "feels precarious" to her, and adds that she won't really feel safe "until the United States has it and it's upheld by the Supreme Court."

Susan Mayne is another teacher who feels insecure despite civil rights protection for gays and lesbians in her state.

> If they want to get rid of you, they can certainly do it in other ways. They're certainly not gonna say, "We're firing you because you're gay." They know it's against the law . . . in Connecticut, anyway.

Sharon teaches in a Washington State school district that prohibits anti-gay discrimination, but she doubts that the clause in her contract would protect her from a determined effort to fire her. "It doesn't necessarily make me feel safer. It does put down on paper what I've always thought would happen anyway."

One of the reasons that legal protection does not always make gay teachers feel safe is that they know they can be pressured or forced to resign without actually being fired. Bill knows a fundamentalist on the school board, who he says "could probably get rid of me pretty quickly if he put the word out to the administration." He doesn't think his administration would fire him; instead, he speculates:

> They'd probably evaluate me to the point where they would be so nitpicky that I'd finally just say, "I've had enough, good-bye." . . . No one would be polite enough to say, "We don't think you're a good influence in our community and you need to go because you're a gay man."

"It's not the fact that they're gonna fire you. It's the process," Susan Mayne agrees. "A principal can kind of watch you. If you're not at your duty or if you're not there, they can make it really uncomfortable. Regardless."

When they talk about their fears of being fired, gay teachers say they think the pressure would be more likely to come from the community than from colleagues or administrators. "Parents have more to fear because they have heard so many rumors about, 'My kid's gonna be recruited,'" says Ruth. "I don't think the teachers really feel that way."

Educators who are liked and respected by the parents of their students wonder how that relationship might change if the parents knew the truth. "I have really good respect [from] most of the parents," says Judi. "I work well with them, I think I'm well respected in the community, and I always ask myself, 'If they knew, would they be my allies still?'" Hope says parents have occasionally told her that they wish their daughters would grow up to be just like her. "And I just sit there and I think, 'No you don't.'"

Bert's worst fantasy is "a group of parents getting really upset and putting pressure" on the headmaster of his school.

I can hear him saying to me, "You know that we value your teaching tremendously. I think you've made a great contribution to the school. I would like to see you stay here. I think the world stinks and I think people are awful; but for the good of the school, I have no choice but to not renew your contract."

"Alice" works with troubled youth at an urban alternative school where most of the students come from dysfunctional families. Her fantasy is less polite and more earthy: "One parent—I can see it now—just looking for anything, coming in and saying, 'Fucking queers work here. They're gonna turn my kid into a queer.'"

The influence of parental opinion is so strong in most communities that even teachers with supportive administrators wonder how long the support would last in the face of community pressure. "My principal could be as supportive as all get out, but . . . parents are very picky in this community," says Rebecca. "The kids, as vicious and cruel as they can be, they can roll with the punches pretty much."

Peggy agrees that administrators often defer to parental complaints, and that parents are often more bigoted than their children.

If I were ever to be fired I imagine it to be happening because the school board comes under political pressure, and I don't think the school board has very much spine. . . . I think kids are so much more enlightened than their parents, and showing such heart and compassion for people and such real willingness to think about what it means to feel like somebody else.

Like Rebecca and Peggy, Valerie enjoys a good relationship with her principal, whom she describes as "a pretty progressive guy." She expects that he would defend her in the face of parental opposition. But she points out:

If administrators have to deal with a lot of negative, negative stuff, it's bound to influence their opinion of you. If you're not doing a perfect job, they're going to start seeing those imperfections all the time, and they're going to be watching. And it's not because they want to see them, it's just because they feel like you're in the spotlight.

Lurking beneath these fears of parental pressure and administrative disapproval is the deeper anxiety that troubles virtually every lesbian or gay educator, the fear of being accused of child abuse. Chris, who has been teaching for over fifteen years, points out that while all teachers worry more than they once did about such accusations, gay men are especially vulnerable.

I can remember a time when I used to come over to students and put my hand on their shoulder when I wanted to talk to them, and that's strictly *verboten*, you know, I'm fearful. . . . Being gay, I'd be even more sensitive of being accused.

Ruth Frobe admits that as an out lesbian in her high school, she is "very conscious of whether or not I touch kids. I always make sure they initiate a hug, or I'll pat kids on the back, or whatever—but I'm hyperconscious of any kind of physical contact with kids whether they know about me or not."

Teachers like Ruth, who are implicitly or explicitly out, can easily fall victim to accusations of pedophilia. During the antigay Measure Nine campaign in Oregon, Michael Scott almost became a target of such accusations. That summer, he had been interviewed on a local TV show about gay rights. Despite the fact that he was shown in shadow and his name was not used, many of his acquaintances recognized him and commented about the show. That year, a student in his computer class accused Mike of "touching him inappropriately." When police questioned the boy, they learned that he had seen Mike on TV the previous summer.

We had meetings with the boy and his father, and at that time he said, "He touches me on the shoulder," and the father asked, "Was that inappropriate?" And fortunately, the father was a very wonderful father, he had talked to his son about inappropriate touching, and the boy said, "No, I was just mad because I got a bad grade." And he apologized to me.

After that, Mike says, he and the boy got along well, but the incident left him feeling very insecure. "I realized just how, if a person wanted to get you, they could. . . . It's just very scary."

Jan Goodman found that during her years as a closeted administrator, her heightened visibility led her to monitor her behavior with students. She recalls, "I noticed that I would put my arms around boys, like I was really pals with all of them—we were walking arm in arm—and girls I never initiated contact with." Bill, too, feels caught between his need to prove himself as an effective administrator and his vulnerability as a gay man working with young children. "I think people see me as being very effective, that I'm kind and I'm gentle with children, [but] I purposely don't do things that look like I'm touching children inappropriately."

Like gay men who work in elementary schools, lesbian P. E. teachers and coaches are conscious of their behavior with students. Pat Tomaso recalls that as a P. E. teacher and public school playground supervisor she was always fearful of accusations.

We had to be very careful, as most teachers do just in general, about being alone with students because straight, gay, or otherwise, you can get accused of molesting children. But I was hypervigilant about this because of my sexual orientation. I even found myself not hugging the kids as much and not being as affectionate to them as they want[ed].

Doralynn, who formerly taught P. E., says she always "made it a point" to take another teacher with her when she was in the locker room with students. Carolyn says that once she realized she was a lesbian, she no longer felt free to coach softball in her rural Michigan community.

If I ever did come out [to the community], that would be one thing they could throw right up in my face. Well, you were in the locker room with the girls. It shouldn't make a difference, but . . . in their minds I know it does.

The stereotype of gay men and lesbians as child molesters persists in spite of dozens of studies showing that between 95 and 98 percent of child sexual abusers are heterosexual men. In recent years, the myth has been kept alive by groups with very specific agendas for religion, sexuality, and the family. Gay teachers are the most visible targets of these right-wing groups, who manipulate public fears about the well-being of families and children under the label of "Christian" values. So it is not surprising that gay men and lesbians teaching in conservative communities or places where fundamentalists have waged political campaigns are especially fearful. Claire is a school counselor in a rural New England district where fundamentalists have already tried to influence school policy in a neighboring town.

If something bad was going to happen, it would be fundamentalist parents [who] would march on the school board and try to get me out. . . . We have a good school board and they would be above that. The underlying problem is that it could diminish my effectiveness as a counselor because . . . parents wouldn't want kids in groups with me.

Chris teaches in a conservative district in rural Iowa. He imagines what might happen if the wrong group of parents learned about his sexual orientation.

I have this fear about having parents go to the school board complaining that they heard that Mr. Marshall is gay, that he's teaching our kids. . . . Some of the parents I work with, probably their fundamentalist beliefs are against homosexuality. They might be outraged at the idea that the school district would hire a homosexual. That's the underlying fear all the time.

Dianne has already heard, indirectly, from some of the fundamentalist parents in her rural community.

> There's this boy I have that I like a lot, a really bright kid. He was talking to another teacher, and he said, "You know, I really like Miss Wilson a lot, but my mother said that if she ever gives me a hassle about anything, that I should tell her what it says in the Bible about queers." I was devastated because I had to go into class an hour and a half every day and look at this kid and get past what I knew.

Gay educators who have survived antigay political campaigns are especially aware of the power of right-wing fundamentalist groups. Bill fears that if he came out more openly as a gay elementary school principal in Colorado Springs, he would be "squeezed pretty hard from lots of people to quit." He adds:

> It would come, at some level, from the churches in the neighborhood where I work—not all the churches, but there are some pretty fundamental kinds of churches there. . . . We have a person from the fundamental community on our school board right now, and that is pretty scary, to think that he could probably get rid of me pretty quickly if he put the word out to the administration.

Barbara and Shirley also teach in Colorado Springs, and feel threatened by the religious right. Shirley has already been warned by the father of a student who received low grades for attendance and behavior.

> His father's a big uppity-up with Focus [Focus on the Family, the conservative Christian group that helped spearhead Colorado's 1992 antigay Amendment Two]. . . . They wanted to make sure that there weren't some other issues involved in my treatment of this boy. I think he was being very subtle, but I think he's heard the rumors, and I don't think he's happy about me particularly and wanted me to understand on some level I better watch my p's and q's with his son.

Barbara acknowledges that the presence of groups like Focus on the Family has made a difference in her teaching.

> I find myself being afraid of religious parents in school. And I never used to be. . . . Now I find myself being more careful in classes where I know that those kids are there. I shouldn't need to feel afraid of them.

Julie has taught for over a decade as a closeted lesbian in Colorado Springs. During the past few years, she has had ample opportunity to observe her colleagues' attitudes toward lesbian and gay teachers. She fears that if she came out to them, these attitudes would automatically attach themselves to her.

> These are people in their late thirties, forties, fifties, and this is really how they feel. They . . . would have nothing to do with me. . . . That's why I can't tell them, because I feel like I would have no friends at all.

Julie's fears are so intense that she cannot even imagine the possibility that her colleagues might rethink their attitudes toward lesbians and gays, rather than reject someone they had worked with for so long. But while her anxieties may be extreme, she is not alone in her fear of public condemnation. Even in communities where political opposition is less organized, the thought of open humiliation is as distressing as the thought of losing a job. Chris says he fears "not so much coming out or being outed, but just having to be dragged through the process. Having to be put on display and listening to people's rantings and ravings. And not knowing what kind of support I would get from other colleagues."

Though the fear of public rejection lurks in many gay teachers' minds, most agree with Allan Gold that "being ridiculed by kids . . . would probably be more painful . . . than [by] the parents. 'Cause parents do it in a more subtle way."

Michael admits to a "paranoid fantasy" of "walking down the hall every day having people whisper as I walk by, or do catcalls." Sharon wonders, "How do you defend yourself when you're in a classroom, you're supposed to be talking about American Lit, and some kid says to you, 'I heard you're a fucking dyke'?"

As most gay teachers recognize, the students most likely to harass them are adolescents in turmoil over their own sexual orientation. Terry Minton remembers his own behavior as a closeted teenager growing up in rural Oklahoma.

> I was a real troublemaker in high school. If I had known a teacher was gay, I would have tortured him to death. And my fear, like most people's fears, is encountering your own self. My God, the worst thing in the world for me [would be] to be a queer teacher and have a kid like me in the class.

Dan Woog admits that the same fear kept him from coming out to his Westport, Connecticut, high school students for a long time.

I was a rabid homophobe in high school. In fact, when I came out, one of my friends from high school said, "Boy, you owe so-and-so a real apology." I said, "Why?" He said, "Because you were brutal to him." This was a guy who, of course, turned out later to be gay as well. And he was right. I was. I pretended to be a jock and I really did everything that I could to hide my homosexuality.

Gay teachers' fear of losing students' respect is so strong that even those who know they cannot be fired for being gay, those with supportive administrations and supportive communities, still hesitate to come out in school. Like Michael, they cannot bear the thought of losing the connection that is their deepest reason for teaching.

When I talk to kids now and I look in their eyes, there's a lot of joy and love, and that's really why I'm there. If that were to change because of who I am, then I don't think I'd want to teach anymore. You know if I looked in kids' eyes and they were giving me a real weird look, or you know, kind of a distant kind of a thing.

As a closeted gay teacher in a suburban high school, Michael has never been targeted by students. But he knows what happened to his gay predecessor, "Curtis."

They would put things on his door, you know, like "This is Curtis the fag's room." They would call him "fag," they would shout it down the hallway. They would call up his phone several times a day. . . . He'd pick it up and [they'd] say, "Fag." . . . My worst-case scenario is that I would be treated the way Curtis was treated.

Michael is afraid to come out to his students because he does not want to be "treated the way Curtis was treated." Yet he acknowledges that Curtis was targeted by students without ever coming out to them; it was his "effeminate" behavior, and not the actual knowledge of his sexual orientation, that provoked the attacks. Michael's story suggests that staying in the closet does not necessarily offer protection from student harassment, and that harassment has as much to do with attitudes about masculinity (and femininity) as with the actual information that someone is lesbian or gay.

Like Michael, Leslie alternates "between being really angry that [coming out] would make me lose my credibility with some kids, to feeling like I'm doing the best thing because I have all their attention and they listen to me."

As an employee of the Denver Public Schools, she is guaranteed job protection based on sexual orientation, yet as a lesbian teaching in Colorado, she can never be sure about the political beliefs of her students and their families.

> When a kid walks through your door, you never know if they have come from a home where they have been told gay people are complete and total perverts. . . . I don't want a kid's prejudicial learning that they have gotten at home to cut me out of their lives so that I cannot impact them in any way, because I believe that my effect on them for the most part is good and positive and lifelong for some. . . . We all want to be accepted and loved for our character, just like Martin Luther King said.

The closer a teacher's relationship with his or her students, the more painful the fear of rejection. Frank has become especially close to four of his sixth-grade boys, who arranged to mow his lawn, plant flowers, and put a big banner on his door as an end-of-the-year present. These boys are only a few of the many students whom he has befriended over the years.

> I take the kids out, and we can go play golf, or go out for pizza. After they've gone to the junior high, they stop by after school and they correct papers for me. . . . Seven o'clock comes around, I'm dropping them off at their homes. I don't want to lose that. . . . I think that's the thing that keeps me in the closet.

The fear that hangs over gay teachers goes beyond being fired, or humiliated, or even rejected by students. Carolyn Wood describes it as "fear of this unknown, scary thing that you're gonna get in big trouble." Tom calls it "a paranoid element in my life." To Laurie, it has to do with vulnerability.

> It's almost like, once you make yourself vulnerable, you can never take that back. And on one level, I don't know what the big deal is about being so vulnerable. Okay, so let them deal with it. But . . . it gives people a lot of power to use against me.

This nameless fear extends far beyond the school building to every corner of a gay teacher's life. It troubles Karen Cosper when she walks to the school parking lot after the girls' basketball games.

> This [rainbow] sticker is on my car, and the parents see me get in my car and drive off, and that's on my mind. . . . I'm not afraid of it being there. But it's still an issue, it's still on my mind.

Terry Minton admits that in his days as a closeted teacher, the fear of discovery extended beyond his own death.

> I used to worry, "My God, what if I'm killed in a car accident, they're going through my artifacts, they find a picture, they find a book, they find something that would indicate that I'm queer." I couldn't even deal with the idea of people after I was dead finding out.

Nancy Goldstein probably comes as close as anyone to identifying the source of her nameless fear when she looks back at her years as a closeted school social worker. "I mean, why was I really worried?" she asks herself. "I wasn't gonna lose my job, probably, I mean—what's the ultimate thing? What do I have to lose, really? What else is it but internalized homophobia?"

Nancy is partly correct in identifying her nameless anxieties as "internalized homophobia." What her analysis leaves out, however, is that every gay teacher has heard stories of real people who were harassed, humiliated, threatened, or fired from their teaching jobs solely because they were gay. For most teachers, these stories are cautionary tales about what can happen to a gay educator. For some, they are more than just stories.

7

Cornered

TO THE AVERAGE HETEROSEXUAL READER, THE FEARS OF LESbian and gay teachers may seem extreme, even paranoid. The truth is that despite the proliferation of gay/straight alliances and diversity days, despite the very real legal and contractual gains of the last ten years, gay teachers are still harassed, humiliated, and fired because they are lesbian or gay. In some cases, the victims are teachers who have dared to come out to colleagues or students, but just as often they have done everything possible to conceal their sexual orientation and have never shared their private lives with anyone.

In schools where the climate is indifferent or hostile to lesbians and gays, students can make life unbearable for a gay teacher. In other cases, parental pressure, narrow-minded colleagues, or intolerant administrators have forced gay teachers to resign or fired them outright. The lesson that runs through all these horror stories is that heterosexual allies—colleagues, parents, administrators, sometimes even students—have tremendous power to help or destroy gay and lesbian teachers. Through their indifference or inaction, they can allow lives and careers to be shattered; yet by their simple advocacy, they can defeat the forces that would turn gay teachers into criminals.

Annette has been teaching physical education at the same inner-city high school for twenty-one years. Despite occasional homophobic incidents early on, she has had a good relationship with her students, and has enjoyed her teaching career. But in recent years, Annette's confidence has been shaken by a series of attacks so intense that she has considered quitting her job.

A few years after Annette joined the faculty, she made what she now considers the great mistake of telling a female basketball player who had come out to her that she too was a lesbian. Not long afterward, Annette walked into the locker room to find that someone had written on all the walls, "MASON'S A LESBIAN." On Valentine's Day that year, she received a note in her mailbox with a picture of herself and a student, kissing.

> That freaked me out. I've never come out to a student again. . . . I just prayed, God, just graduate, just get the hell out of here so I don't have to be dealing with this.

A few years later, Annette was confronted by a student in one of her classes.

> It was springtime and we were going around the track and the school windows were all open. She was mad at me, I can't remember what it was over, but anyway, I was down at the other end of the track and every time she came around this end she was yelling at the top of her lungs, "My teacher's a dyke." Just at the top of her lungs yelling this.

Luckily, the girl's counselor was someone Annette felt comfortable coming out to.

> I said, "I don't know what to do. She's calling me a dyke. I am. I don't know how to handle this other than she needs to be out of my class so I don't have to deal with this on a daily basis." And so then she was taken out of the class.

In recent years, attacks against Annette have increased. The worst harassment came from a girl who had failed her class.

> One of the deans came down and called her out of class, and I guess her mother had just gotten her report card and chewed her out over the phone. She came back to my class, and it's still in session. She started calling me "faggot" and "lesbian." . . . I was trying to run interference like a radio, and just kind of tune this out. . . . I went up to her and she just kept going on, and I said, "Well, you're gonna need to leave right now."

Annette called the dean to remove the girl from class, but did not feel comfortable coming out to an administrator. She assured the dean that she was not a lesbian, and tried to focus on the girl's disruptive behavior. "Of course that made me feel shitty having to deny."

When the girl came back a few days later, she continued to harass Annette, finally throwing a volleyball at her. Annette phoned the girl's mother. "The mother said, 'Yeah, she's calling you "lesbian" and "faggot," she calls you a faggot.' And I kept trying to bring it back to her grades."

By this time, Annette says, she felt "like the deer on the road with the headlights on . . . absolutely cornered." Two final encounters in the locker room shook her confidence even further.

> While I was in the storage closet I heard somebody say to this other girl, "Why'd you say that? Why'd you go and say that about Ms. Mason?" And when I came out and invited the girl to come down and get her lock, she says, "I'm not going with you. I'm not coming downstairs with you." . . . And so here I was again, kind of trapped. And just about a month ago I was coming down through the locker room. . . . I unlocked the door from the inside and came out and somebody said, "Homo, hey dude," like that, to me, and I thought, I can't do this any more, I can't stay here any more.

By the middle of the year, Annette had decided that she needed to "start over, start new somewhere else." But during the second semester, she met some students who changed her mind.

> I was blessed with two P. E. classes of girls who were the best by far in all my twenty years. I've never enjoyed myself or my students so much. They were kind to one another and me. They were fun loving and appreciative. As a result of their goodness, I have decided to stay. I even told these students that I had been planning to leave until they came into my life.

Annette acknowledges that "homophobia may, or most probably will rear its ugly head again." She is "taking it one year at a time," hoping that "the worst homophobia is in the past." But the atmosphere at her school remains hostile, abetted by an administration that does not defend its lesbian and gay students or teachers. All of this is made worse, Annette believes, by the climate in the world outside. "The issue is so much out there now," she says. "They have a green light to express their hatred for gay people."

Rebecca is another teacher who has faced student harassment, but for her, the support of an administrator turned things around. One spring morning, she arrived at school to find her file drawer overflowing with toilet paper.

> I thought that was weird. So I dug a little further and underneath the toilet paper was a paper cup. Written in bold black marker [was] "We hate you, Miss Harris, dyke from hell," and on my desk calendar blotter written across the top was "DYKE."

That night, shocked and angry, Rebecca shared the incident with her partner.

I told her, "I've got to do something." I said, "It may mean my job, it may mean—I'm not sure what it means." She was very supportive and said, "You've gotta do this."

Armed with the evidence of the calendar and the paper cup, Rebecca went to her principal.

I showed him the cup and he said, "I can't believe this, this upsets me so. I'm so upset." We discussed homosexuality among students, that there are definitely some at our school, and finally narrowing the gap to zero in on me, with him saying, "You know, Rebecca I don't know what your sexual preference is. I think I know, but I don't know for sure. It doesn't matter to me." . . . He's a very serious, somber, large-framed guy who you could have a very weak feeling about, that he could be extremely homophobic. The "good ole New Hampshire boy," born and raised. . . . I said, "If you think I'm a lesbian, you're right." He said, "I knew you were when I hired you."

Before school ended in June, Rebecca went to see her principal again. Together, they began planning a school diversity team, which would work to end racism, sexual harassment, and other kinds of discrimination, including homophobia. The principal asked Rebecca to help lead the team, and she is already compiling a list of guest speakers, including members of the local gay and lesbian youth group. Looking back on the events of the spring, she asserts that what was most significant was not the student harassment, but the principal's response. "It's been probably the most tumultuous [period] of my life because of actually opening this and having my principal say, 'I knew it when I hired you and it has nothing to do with you being a teacher.'"

David Bruton was the target of more than just verbal harassment at Chapel Hill High School, where he teaches English. Several years ago, an appeal from a former student prompted David to organize a discussion on lesbian and gay issues as part of a schoolwide diversity series.

Our advisory group got a letter from a boy who said he wished that we would talk about homosexuality, because if there had been somebody that he could have talked to, he probably wouldn't have tried to commit suicide the year that he did. . . . And you know, when a kid says "I might not have tried to commit suicide if I could talk," it just sort of does something to one.

Although he was not officially out in his school, David volunteered to set up the discussion, and helped students post flyers around school. Shortly afterwards, the flyers disappeared and someone shot through the windows of David's second-floor classroom with a BB gun.

And then the BB's didn't do a good enough job, so I came in one Monday morning and there was a big rock hurled through the window. . . . And they replaced the window, and I thought, "Well, still, it's just vandalism." . . . And then one day they broke it out and threw a dead possum through the window.

At about this time, several drop-off boxes for a PTA clothing drive were burned, and David's name was sprayed around the ashes. His name was also spray painted all over the school buses.

It said something like "Bruton's a fag. Fire Bruton." The school-bus coordinator claimed he didn't know who that was, so he just let the buses roll all over the school district. Several teachers saw it . . . as they were coming into school . . . and called the central office and literally raised hell.

At last, school officials were able to identify the perpetrators, who turned out to be three of David's students.

Two of them . . . are having a great deal of difficulty in proving to everyone that they're men, and unfortunately the third one is gay and he was having to go along to cover. . . . I think that's one of the shames of this whole thing. What this kid had to do to himself in order to be able to hold his head up.

All three students eventually were permitted to complete their classes and graduate. Though none of them ever apologized, one, who was in David's homeroom, apparently grew to respect the teacher he had once harassed. "At the end of the year just before he went in to the graduation line, he came over and shook my hand. That was all." David's compassion for the struggles of gay youth makes him sorrowful, rather than angry, when he thinks about the incident. "You know, when you look at the travail and the effort that gay people go through to hold their head up, it's enough to make you cry."

But David's life at school during this period was not entirely bleak. A group of students whom he calls his "protective squad" began checking in with him every day to make sure everything was all right. "One of them told me flat out, 'Look, if you want us to take care of 'em, we will.'" Teachers and administrators expressed support, and, after he wrote an op-ed piece for the local newspaper, so did many in the community. "A lot of people just couldn't stand the fact that something was happening to somebody that they didn't think it should happen to, regardless of what their sexual orientation was."

Most gratifying of all, David Bruton's ordeal inspired other gay students and faculty at Chapel Hill High School. David recalls a new teacher, a gay man who came into his room one morning full of anxiety. David reassured him, saying, "Look, if you are a decent human being and you teach the kids what they need to know, you respect them as human beings, you can be green and they'll still accept you for what you are." The new teacher was so encouraged that he added his name to the list of sponsors for the school's Gay/Straight Alliance.

Harassment by a student escalated to an even more violent level for Carolyn, a social studies teacher at a K–12 school of four hundred students in rural Michigan. The student who threatened her was a fifteen-year-old freshman with a troubled background. His father, who had been accused of beating the boy's mother, had left the family and was rumored to be a member of the Ku Klux Klan. Carolyn describes the boy as "one of the ones, the solution to every crime problem was, 'Kill 'em, kill 'em, kill 'em.'" When the topic in Carolyn's social studies class turned to current gay rights campaigns, "his comments just got more and more outrageous." Once, after Carolyn had been absent from school, she learned that the boy had stood up in class and announced that Carolyn was having an affair with a female student, and that the student was a lesbian. The girl's parents demanded to know what was going to be done, but when Carolyn reported the incident to the administration, they did nothing.

Carolyn's principal had already made her life difficult during his five years at her school. "I'd gotten 'excellent' to 'very satisfactory' ratings from every administrator till he came," she says, "and his very first evaluation of me was 'unsatisfactory.' . . . One of the comments he made was that I needed to wear more dresses." He had also forbidden her to show the film *And the Band Played On* as part of a curriculum unit on government bureaucracy, because "it showed two males kissing."

Frustrated by the principal's inaction, Carolyn confronted the boy who had harassed her and warned him about the danger of spreading rumors. The boy immediately accused her of "threatening" him. But for Carolyn, the "threatening" had only begun.

> The following Monday, they had a class assignment where they had to write about crime. . . . One of the crimes was carrying a concealed weapon. And he wrote this story about following me home and blowing my head off with a concealed weapon, which, once you pull it out is no longer concealed. He had basically taken the assignment as a chance to really lay it on me.

Carolyn again appealed to her principal, and met with the boy's mother, but again the boy went unpunished. "They said that they'd take it seriously if it happened again. But no suspension, nothing. I was livid."

Carolyn decided to make a police report on her own, "just because I didn't feel safe." She also inquired about prosecuting the student under Michigan's stalking law, but was told that he would have to do something more overt before a stalking warning could be issued. A week later, the boy left his class during a school field trip, went into a department store, and was caught shoplifting shotgun shells. For this he was sentenced to a three-day suspension. By now, says Carolyn, she was "very, very concerned."

> Basically he stopped talking to me. You know, he didn't say anything but it was just these hateful looks all day in class. He was in my class this year too, repeating the course, because I am the only social studies teacher. And he basically didn't say anything, and when he did say things, it was borderline neo-Nazi crap. . . . A lot of comments I felt were directed at me.

Carolyn contacted her union representative, who knows she is a lesbian. While the union rep was very sympathetic, she told Carolyn that if she wanted to take action, she would have to come out publicly. Unfortunately, that was something Carolyn was not ready to do, especially since the boy's father lived in her hometown.

Many of Carolyn's colleagues, who knew of her sexual orientation, were outraged about the situation, but no one seemed to know what to do, especially since the principal would not take any leadership. His timidity reinforced the boy's bravado. "He bragged about it because he got away with it. Nothing happened, he didn't get suspended."

To Carolyn's relief, the year ended without further incident, and the student remained "very, very quiet most of the time . . . He still let me know he didn't like me." To her even greater relief, the whole family moved away the following year.

> They're joining some religious organization down south, and they're moving into a commune down there. . . . I was relieved. I mean, it's terrible to go into an environment where you feel like you're being personally threatened.

Carolyn holds her administration responsible for the escalation of the threats against her. She adds an interesting footnote about her principal, who has finally left the school.

> I found out after he left that he has a daughter who's a lesbian. . . . His daughter had lived out of town, and apparently his wife had a real hard time with his daughter's life-style.

Carolyn is thinking about moving to a more cosmopolitan area. Despite her ordeal—or perhaps because of it—she wants to come out before she leaves, to "kind of complete my story. . . . My coming out, one way or the other, is going to be educational," she says. "I think there's a pretty good shot I will."

Carolyn's and Annette's stories show how a weak or indifferent administration can create a climate where students feel free to target lesbian and gay teachers. Some gay teachers have had even more difficult experiences with administrators. Ruth Frobe is an athletic director and physical education teacher at Orting High School, in a town she describes as a "conservative, redneck" suburb of Seattle, Washington. In 1994, after years of harassment by her principal, she filed an affirmative action complaint charging that he had referred to her behind her back as "the dyke A. D. [Athletic Director]" and "the queer in that office."

Later that year, a parent named Mary Peck, who happened to be standing outside the doorway of Ruth's office, noticed a small postcard amid the many posters and flyers on the door. A favorite in women's studies offices and women's centers, the card is headed "How to be a Fabulous Feminist," and includes a host of suggestions, from "Help a Mother Today," to "Elect Progressive Women," to "Honor Lesbians." Without informing Ruth or anyone else, Peck copied down the text of the postcard and sent it to several conservative state representatives, who immediately contacted Ruth's principal.

At a school-board meeting convened to discuss the matter, six parents spoke against Ruth, including a man who called the sign "propaganda that encourages unnatural things." Ruth spoke last. She told the board:

> I was raised by heterosexual parents, and went to school with heterosexual teachers. Do you think one lesbian in your high school is going to make kids gay? It's pretty obvious this is about more than just a postcard.

Mary Peck denied that her concerns had anything to do with Ruth's sexual orientation. She assured a Tacoma *News Tribune* reporter, "I do not mind in any way, shape, or form her personal choice," adding, "She wears men's clothes, a man's watch. Her haircut is shorter than my husband's, who's in the Army."

Ruth had already decided to quit her position as athletic director in favor of full-time teaching. She agreed not to post the sign in her classroom. She is also looking for another job. But she does not regret being out at her school. "I think it's ludicrous that a postcard made it to the front page of the Tacoma *News Tribune*," she says, "but in a way it's cool, since no one is willing to talk about the real issue except me." Ruth adds that her students have been almost universally supportive. "They all want copies of the postcard for their rooms," she says.

Three thousand miles away, a hostile administrator drove Timothy Brown out of his classroom and halfway across the country. Tim had received excellent evaluations until the night he went to an AIDS benefit at a gay bar.

> Someone—and I still don't know who, probably will never know—wrote down my faculty parking sticker number and my license number, and so began the witch-hunt that lasted eighteen months.

Tim received harassing calls on his answering machine and was followed home by supervisors who sat in their cars near his house. Abruptly, his evaluations changed. "I had suddenly become very incompetent. I didn't know how to write lesson plans. I had no sense of discipline and, you know, it just went on from there."

At about this time, Tim broke up with his lover, and lost a great deal of weight.

> I was going in for tests to find out why I was losing all this weight, and of course, no one ever said it could be stress. I had a blood test . . . and the vein in my arm broke once and made this purple thing on my arm. . . . People asked me if that was from my AIDS test. I told them it was none of their business. It wasn't from an AIDS test but it was inappropriate of them to ask that to start with.

At the end of that year, Tim was denied tenure. School district employees are not protected from antigay discrimination in the district where he was teaching, and state law does not require official justification for the termination of a probationary teacher. Although his lawyer thought he might have a legal case based on the AIDS baiting, "proving they thought I had AIDS was even more difficult than proving they thought I was gay."

So Tim left the district and the state, and started over in Colorado. He now teaches at an inner-city high school, where the students "are used to minority issues." Even so, it has taken him years to feel relaxed in his present school. "Every time a principal would walk in my room or say something to me, I would be terrified," he says of his early days in the district. "Every time I had contact with a parent, I was really nervous. . . . It took me a while to get over that."

Tim has settled out of court with his previous district and is happy with the new life he has built for himself. But he has not forgotten the students at his other school. "They gave me 'The World's Best Teacher' shirt when I left, and 'The World's Best Teacher' coffee mug, and they signed a concert poster for me, and framed it." There is a catch in his voice, and a long pause, before Tim goes on to talk about other classes, and other students.

Tim is not the only gay teacher who has found himself the object of AIDS-phobic suspicions. "Larry," a high school teacher in the southwest, was forced out of his first teaching job for the same reason. To make things worse, in his case, the suspicions were true.

> I graduated when I was nineteen and started teaching. I had senior govern-
> ment, and so those kids were seventeen and eighteen, and it was real
> hard. . . . That was the time I found out I was positive. . . . I was basically
> asymptomatic, but I lost a lot of weight, I think worrying—worry, stress of
> my first year of teaching, coaching two seasons. And I think it kind of got
> rumored, and I was given a very, very hard time.

Without warning, Larry's principal accused him of cursing in front of students, being "inappropriate" with female members of his team, and not "handling [him]self appropriately as a teacher." The accusations continued until eventually, Larry resigned. Neither sexual orientation nor AIDS was ever mentioned, but Larry is convinced "that was the bottom line." Happily, he was able to find a more congenial teaching job in another district, and remains optimistic—and asymptomatic—eight years later.

Few teachers have as gruesome a story to tell as "Peter," a Catholic school teacher in the New York City area. Peter had not even begun his teaching job at a private Catholic high school when he received a call from the principal. There on the principal's desk was an anonymous letter of the most obscene variety, targeting Peter as a homosexual and signed, "God Bless You." Peter, who had only recently left a religious order and was barely out even to himself, was stunned. For the next four months, similar letters continued to arrive at the offices of the principal and vice principal, all typed and unsigned, and all mailed from different parts of the country. Peter was too terrified to contact the police, and the school had no teachers union. "I just wanted it to go away," he says.

Meanwhile, Peter's work life became increasingly unbearable. He describes the school as "a nut factory," largely because of the "crazy and controlling" habits of the principal, who insisted that all cars in the teachers parking lot be parked facing the same way, and reprimanded Peter for wearing the wrong kind of socks to student lacrosse practice. Peter's relationship with his students, on the other hand, was wonderful. He especially enjoyed the "C-track kids"—"the grunts," he calls them—with whom he developed an excellent rapport.

At last, calling the situation "a bomb ticking," the principal notified the authorities about the letters. Almost immediately, Peter was summoned to an investigation that had nothing to do with his case. He was brought to a lineup and asked if he could identify a man accused (and later convicted) of child molestation. Peter had never seen the man before. To this day, he wonders, "Why did they pick me?"

In November, the letters abruptly ceased. Nothing was ever said about them again, but Peter was clearly under suspicion. "Every time I went in the office, there was the subtle implication: 'Nothing had better happen.'"

Peter remained at the school, and in the closet, for another five years. Then one Sunday afternoon, something snapped. As advisor to the yearbook, Peter was expected to work on weekends as well as after school. He had asked to take Saturday off to attend the funeral of an old friend who had died of AIDS. The principal refused to approve his request, demanding, "Who was this, anyway?"

Peter says, "This was the last straw." On Monday morning, he appeared in the principal's office, and told him to "have a nice life." The following afternoon, he returned to clean out his room.

For a while after that, it looked as though things would only get worse. Teaching jobs were nowhere to be found, Peter was drinking more and arguing with his lover, and eventually the lover moved out of their apartment. One night that winter, Peter was reading a bedtime story to his niece, a story about love. Suddenly, he found himself starting to cry. He poured out his heart to his sister, the first person in his family to learn that he was gay. Instead of condemning him, as he had feared, she told Peter that she loved him.

Exactly one year after the death of his old friend, whose funeral had precipitated Peter's abrupt departure from "the nuthouse," Peter received a call from one of the many school districts where he had applied for jobs. He is now teaching junior and senior English, and enjoys a good relationship with students and staff, and, most important, with the administration. Soon after he began his new job, Peter ran into one of his colleagues at a gay AA meeting. He is Peter's first real ally in his teaching life, "someone with whom I don't have to hide."

Peter's experiences have left scars that may never disappear. He scrupulously guards his identity, and will not be interviewed on tape. Even so, he talks hopefully about the future. He even sees himself coming out to more people—"very slowly and very carefully." "You know," he says, "I never would have done this interview two years ago."

In the winter of 1993, Oregon's lesbian and gay teachers were still recovering from the campaign over Ballot Measure Nine, which had threatened to deny all legal protection to the state's lesbian and gay citizens. That February, Sue was working with the NAMES project to bring the AIDS quilt to her Portland middle school. The Quilt had special meaning for Sue; one of the panels bore the name of her brother, who had died of AIDS five years earlier.

As soon as word got out that the Quilt was coming to school, tensions began to rise. They were stirred by a husband and wife, both teachers at Sue's school and both active members of the Oregon Citizen's Alliance, the antigay group that had campaigned in favor of Ballot Measure Nine.

> They rallied the community to get all upset about the whole thing. . . . The principal was in conferences with parents for two and three hours after school because they were so upset about the Quilt being there. The husband was taking pictures of the Quilt and sending it to the O.C.A. headquarters saying, "This is the homosexual agenda in our building, it's happening here, you've got to see this."

The morning of the unfolding, Sue and another teacher looked at the panels. On one, they noticed a photograph of a man in a leather G-string, which they agreed was "probably inappropriate" for middle schoolers. Sue and her colleague taped some paper over the photograph and brought the Quilt down to the gym.

Sue recalls the unfolding itself as "an incredible ceremony."

> I mean, five hundred, six hundred kids packed into that gym. And it was the quietest I've ever heard that many middle schoolers. We had some media there. We had invited parents and some other adults, friends, and that sort of thing.

During the ceremony, NAMES Project volunteers read the names on the panels.

> Then I said that we could open the microphone for anybody who wanted to come down and say the name of somebody that they knew who had died of AIDS, and I started. The last name I read was my brother's name, and that was the first time that I'd ever revealed that to everybody.

Later on, the quilt was hung in the school library, with the piece of paper still taped over the questionable photograph.

> One of the teachers, the wife of the husband-and-wife team, took her class into the library. . . . We hadn't put a barrier in front of the Quilt at this point, and the kids . . . didn't follow the "Don't touch" rules and they saw the piece of paper and took it off. They saw the picture and went into little fits, and ran to their teacher, and she went over and saw it and she threw a

wild fit. . . . She went to the office and said the whole thing was inappropriate, that kids were being exposed to all of this stuff that was awful. . . . Word got to me by the next period and I was furious. . . . We got a barrier put up in front of it but the damage had been done by that time.

During another assembly, while everyone was in the school auditorium, the man Sue calls "Mr. O.C.A." secured a school camera and went to the library. "He started photographing the quilt, and I think he pulled the paper off at the same time and took a picture of that."

Because of the commotion, the principal decided to have a round-table meeting "to air everybody's feelings." The husband and wife complained that the Quilt should have been approved by the entire staff and that it was part of "a homosexual agenda that we were pushing in the school." Other teachers made trivial or irrelevant comments.

I was the only one in there who was being real. I said that this had not been an agenda, there was no political motive behind this at all, that the whole focus was trying to teach kids about AIDS and what choices they needed to make. . . . it was something on an emotional level and then I lost it and started crying and I couldn't stop.

To her surprise, Sue found that not all the staff members agreed with "Mr. and Mrs. O.C.A."

My principal was right there with her arm around me and the other person sitting next to me was right there, and I had a lot of support. And as I spoke I think the women teachers were pretty moved emotionally. There were other people that were in tears also.

Even more important to Sue, the students at her school understood the meaning of the Quilt.

I got copies of what kids wrote in their journals, and they were really incredible. I mean, the kids got the message. . . . And in some of the journals the kids said that, well, I didn't even know that Ms. Block had lost her brother.

Since the Quilt incident, Sue has moved to another school, where the climate seems more friendly and the staff seems "more professional." As a new teacher in the building she is staying "low-key" for the time being. But when she is asked whether her experience with the AIDS Quilt will keep her in the closet, she quickly responds, "I expect to be more out."

8

"He Handed Me a Letter..."

LESBIANS AND GAY MEN WHO HAVE BEEN HARASSED BY STU-
dents, colleagues, or members of the community rely on supportive allies and
their own courage and determination to help them survive. For some, however, courage and determination are not enough. Their stories show that
despite the gains of the past decade, outright discrimination still threatens gay
teachers in America's schools.

Linda was teaching science at a junior high school in north central
Maine when her ordeal began.

> There were a couple of kids who were cheating on a test blatantly. . . . So I
> told them they would both get zeros and they needed to come in after
> school and I forget what else. There had also been an incident on the play-
> ground . . . where somebody was talking about "one of those fags with a
> limp wrist," and that he was a real sicko. . . . I said people who are gay are
> not necessarily sick. . . . One of the girls went home and in the process of
> telling her mother that she had flunked the test for me, I think [she] must
> have softened that blow with telling this story about how I liked queer peo-
> ple so I obviously must be one.

Although the girl's mother complained to the principal, no further
action was taken, and the incident seemed closed. At the end of her second
year, Linda received tenure. Meanwhile, the girl in question had gone to live
with an aunt and uncle in another town. The following year, Linda's third, the
student returned to the local high school.

I wrote the kid a note when she came back and gave it to a friend of hers to give it to her. "I heard you were back. It would be great to see you. Drop by the school sometime. Hope you're doing all right." The mother got that note. I don't think the girl ever knew I had written it. But the mother decided that . . . I was trying to come on to her daughter. . . . She went straight to the superintendent . . . with this note saying that I was obviously trying to come on to her daughter and that I should be fired for that.

The superintendent accused Linda of bad teaching.

I got a whole bunch of letters fired off to me about how I was never to be with students alone in my classes at any time other than when I was teaching. . . . He was never willing to be specific and put down on paper what it was that I was being accused of. . . . The things he wrote in these letters, which all went straight into my personal file, were things like, "People who work in radical causes are never properly prepared with their classes." It was really off-the-wall. He had never been in to see my classes. He had never seen my lesson plan book. . . . In fact, as far as he and the principal knew, the only social activism I did was that I volunteered with the Boy Scouts and the Girl Scouts.

As pressure mounted over the summer, Linda waited to find out if the school board would remove her from her job. Her union representative, purportedly her ally, proved to be part of the problem.

The feeling of the people in the union both at the local level and . . . within the state was, "Oh well, you got caught. You are not supposed to be friends with kids." . . . He started telling me about this gay male teacher who he knew, who, whenever gossip started going in the community, he made sure he was seen with some woman who was a real good looker.

Isolated and demoralized, Linda gave in.

I felt like my own ideal—which was, if I worked hard enough and did a really good job and was the best that I could possibly be, then people would like me and I would be fine—was an illusion. . . . So I quit. It was awful. I felt numb. I couldn't believe it had happened.

Linda left teaching, left the country, and returned determined to teach again. After taking some science courses at a nearby college, she was able to reconstruct her resumé and found a job at a high school in another district. There, she has built a new career as a capable and popular teacher. Like many gay teachers who have been targeted, Linda's experiences convinced her that her survival depended on being more open about her identity, rather than less. Most of her students now know she is a lesbian.

Thinking back, Linda acknowledges that the differences between her two teaching experiences came mostly from the differences between the schools themselves: one, a small junior high school in a conservative, rural, fundamentalist community; the other, a midsize high school in a coastal town whose large tourist population makes it relatively cosmopolitan. But she is convinced that her efforts to lie about her sexual identity at the junior high school made her more vulnerable.

> I'm convinced that people pick up when you are nervous. They smell blood just like sharks. They know that you are uncomfortable about something and they can't put their finger on just quite what it is. But they know there is something. They would rather just know, I think.

Most gay teachers who are implicitly or explicitly out would agree with Linda that projecting a defensive image can make a teacher more vulnerable. Though they know that confidence alone does not guarantee protection, gay teachers who have been targeted have found that their best hope lies in openly defending themselves. Karen is a lesbian teacher who was "implicitly out" when a group of parents tried to remove her; Michelle Serries and Mary were openly gay teachers when they were attacked. Though they could not control the forces against them, these three women say that no amount of targeting could be worse than the closet.

Karen teaches seventh and eighth grade at a rural elementary school in Maine. Her troubles began when she gave low grades to some eighth-grade basketball players.

> It had never happened in the history of the school. . . . There was a big out-cry. There were three kids who were disqualified from playing. . . . Two of the parents were very upset and decided I hated boys and that was why their sons were gotten off the ball team.

After two boys' parents filed a complaint against her, the principal informed Karen that the parents were holding a secret meeting with the superintendent.

> He said, "It seems to do with the fact that some people think you're a lesbian." I said, "I didn't see a NO DYKES sign when I came across the bridge in Lakeville." And he said, "Well, don't worry about it, it is going to be okay." Well, I decided it probably wasn't going to be okay.

Karen turned to two allies, an art teacher in her building, and a parent who offered to gather support.

> [The parent] went home and called some people, some other people made calls, the ripple effect. When these four people and their children showed up that afternoon to complain to the superintendent, there were nineteen parents and their children to say, "Over our dead bodies you get rid of this woman." It was really wonderful, it really was. Here were these people just being real shits—and all this outpouring of, "We know a good teacher when we see it."

Later that week, Karen received additional supportive phone calls, including one that she relates with some irony.

> One of the people who had lived there twenty years called me up. Funny thing is, she is terribly homophobic. Because she didn't believe what she had heard—she only knew I was a good teacher—she said, "Karen, I just wanted to let you know that they called us communists twenty years ago when we moved here. They don't have a clue what *communist* means and they still call us communists. So don't worry about what they call you." Of course she really didn't know I was a lesbian, but that's beside the fact.

Later that spring, another incident put Karen in jeopardy. Several fifth-grade girls confided to her that their teacher had a habit of "running his hands down a little girl's blouse." When her report to the principal brought no results, Karen threatened to call the state child protection services.

> This teacher was accused by me, the woman who hates men. The woman who wanted to get rid of all the men in the building, the woman who hates boys and is now the woman who hates men. . . . When I told [the principal] that I was going to report to the Department of Human Services, he said, "Do you want to keep your job? Are you planning on staying here?" I said, "Are you threatening me?" And he said, "Oh, no, I thought you were saying you were getting another job."

Despite her vulnerability, Karen continued her efforts to bring the accused molester to justice and refused to resign. She believes that only direct action can force attackers to back down, and that a good network of allies can create a "ripple effect," as she puts it. "These people aren't used to people who pull them out into the light when they are dishonest." Karen's image of bringing her enemies out into the light is a fit metaphor for her own refusal to disappear. In the years following these events, a new principal has taken over, more evidence has surfaced against the alleged molester, and Karen has managed to get tenure, "much to everyone's surprise, I suspect."

> For no good reason people maliciously attacked me. I don't understand. But I won! Maybe justice does prevail! And we'll get rid of that child molester! He's been stealing out of lobster traps, he may end up dead anyway.

At last report, Karen was tacitly out to the administration and staff, and her health had improved dramatically. Best of all, the child molester was finally gone, not as a result of any foul play, but because, at long last, he had retired.

Michelle Serries is a Denver activist who has been a drama coach, school-board candidate, and middle school teacher. She left the Denver Public Schools in 1993, after a series of events in which her identity as an openly lesbian public school teacher provoked a successful effort to fire her.

Michelle's first full-time teaching job was at an alternative junior high school, where she was hired to teach English and drama. Her openness about her sexual orientation gave her a strong rapport with her students, but it led to immediate conflicts with her staff and administration.

> The kids were fine with it. I never heard that any parents called. But the administrators—oh, my God. It was kind of a pain in the butt working with the adults 'cause they were so hung up. But, you know what? It was an opportunity to kind of educate them too, and I really tried to.

As part of her campaign to educate her colleagues, Michelle invited them to a bonding ceremony that she and her partner were planning.

> I got written up for that. The principal tried to make a big deal out of it. He said, "You cannot be handing these things out on school time." I said, "Well, actually, I've been handing them out at the end of the school day." He put one in my file, and I told him to take it out.

Michelle's life at this school reached a climax through a comedy of misunderstandings that reads like the scenario for a Marx Brothers movie.

> One day the students had decided to have a "wear-your-pajamas-to-school day." So I wore regular clothes, but I wore my bathrobe over them. I was working with some girls in the auditorium. They had turned on the blue and the green [lights], so it was kind of this evening look. . . . We were sitting on the stage, all in our bathrobes and slippers, and two of the girls were sitting in front of me and one of them had her head in the lap of the other,

which is a very normal, typical adolescent thing to do. We're sitting there, and I was telling them about the video [about AIDS] we were gonna go see, because the principal asked us to kind of prep the kids on it. . . . So, this secretary opens the auditorium door, and . . . she gets this idea that I'm on the stage in the dark with these young girls, and she sees the two girls with one's head in the lap of the other, closes the door, goes running back downstairs to her office, and tells her supervisor that I am in the auditorium teaching the girls how to be lesbians.

Michelle was confronted with a written accusation, which she denied in a statement of her own. Meanwhile, "Marilyn," a new principal, came into the school, a woman whom Michelle describes as "my worst nightmare." Michelle started receiving written reprimands for infractions that had nothing to do with reality. In one case, she was written up by a custodian who complained that chairs were being thrown in her room. "It was not my room. It was the room next door, and I found out from the head custodian that Marilyn had approached him and said, 'I want you to write this up.' It was a setup."
Michelle was also written up for chronic lateness.

She had to scrounge for this one. She went back and by her calculations I had a total of three minutes of tardiness over a four month period, and she wrote me up on that and gave me a written warning that if I continued to be late, my job was in jeopardy.

The final incident came when Michelle left six students in her room for a moment while she went to get some paper. When she returned, she saw one of the students "glowering" at the front of the room, with an eraser mark on his shirt. By the next day, Michelle had been written up in a letter "that made it sound like I had been out of my classroom for twenty or thirty minutes, leaving a whole class unattended. . . . This kid had been 'assaulted,' so it made it sound like he'd been hospitalized." Michelle was never questioned; because she had been out of her classroom, the union refused to pursue her grievance.
After a three-month medical leave, Michelle was hired at another Denver middle school, where, unfortunately, the infamous Marilyn appeared as assistant principal during her first year. There, too, Michelle was accused of inappropriate conduct. This time the accusation concerned a piece of writing with an "incredibly explicit description of heterosexual sex," which had been composed by a student from Michelle's class and duplicated on the school copy machine. The principal was convinced that Michelle was responsible.

This is the result of my telling kids that I'm gay, for some kid to write something explicit about heterosexual sex. Anyway, he said, "You're out of here," and I had a few minutes to grab whatever I could from my classroom, and I was gone—a full-time, contracted, tenured teacher.

Ultimately, Michelle Serries decided to resign from the Denver Public Schools. While she blames her dismissal on the general ignorance and bigotry of the administration and some of the staff, she thinks Marilyn, the administrator who followed her from one school to the other, was primarily responsible. In fact, Michelle says, she always felt there was something "fishy" about Marilyn.

She seemed to pick out these young women to kind of befriend her, and I always thought there was something a little bit funny about that. . . . The head custodian, who is a really cool guy, he told me one time, "You know what I think the problem is with you and Marilyn? She's jealous of the fact that you're so open." I said, "What do you mean?" And he goes, "I think she's a closet queer."

Although she is no longer teaching middle school, Michelle has no regrets about her openness. "I think it was good for the students, and I think in a way it was good for a lot of the staff as well." If she had it to do over, would she still be as open? "I'd still be out," Michelle says firmly. "I'd still be out."

Being out to students has never been difficult for Mary, who was suddenly placed on involuntary paid leave from her position as a high school English teacher at a school for the Deaf. Like Michelle Serries, Mary was completely comfortable as an out lesbian during her first year of teaching. In Mary's case, the attack came from parents who did not believe a lesbian should be teaching their children.

During her first year at the school, Mary was assigned two notoriously difficult freshman classes. Despite her initial frustration with the students' behavior, she developed a good relationship with them, fostered by her honesty. She was not afraid to tell her students that she was a lesbian, that she had a partner, that she and her partner had broken up, and that she had two sons just a little younger than her students. Not until December did Mary receive a hint that there might be a problem.

One of my students came up to me after class and she said, "Oh, I'm really worried about my mother. My mother is a very strong Christian . . . and my mother would never let me come to school here if she thought any of my teachers were not in line with what we believe." And I thought, "Why is she saying this to me?"

Mary reassured the girl, "Oh, I've met your mother. I don't think there's any problem. I think everything's fine." But she started to feel uneasy.

The next week she was absent. . . . And I was so scared that something had gone on, her mother had found out, had pulled her out of the school. . . . And then she came back the following week. And I was like, Oh, thank God.

No one said anything more about Mary's suitability as a teacher until the third week in May, when she was unexpectedly called into the superintendent's office in the middle of the school day.

He handed me a letter that said I was being put on administrative leave with pay, pending an investigation of allegations of misconduct and unprofessional behavior. . . . I asked him for an explanation of what that meant, and he said he couldn't say anything further than what was in the letter at that time, and that I was to be escorted off campus.

Mary was told to collect her belongings, turn in her keys, and leave the building. Included in the letter was a statement that she was not to have any contact with students without prior permission. She was also told that she would be called to a meeting, at which time she would be told what the allegations were.

Needless to say [I was] very upset. I had no idea. I had my two kids to come home to, and how—what am I going to say to them? I didn't even know what to say I was charged with because I didn't know.

After a meeting was scheduled and then abruptly cancelled, Mary was summoned to a second meeting a week and a half later. At the meeting were the superintendent and the principal, along with Mary and her union representative. She also insisted on bringing a colleague, another lesbian teacher in her school.

My union representative started by saying that since I had no idea what the allegations were, and they were about to interrogate me, could we at least see the questions and have a few minutes to consult before having to answer. And they said no, but they would give me the categories. So they gave me five categories, which were, inappropriate language, talking about my personal life, classroom control issues, drugs, and student favoritism.

The administrators said Mary had used foul language to her students (she did admit that she had used a few four-letter words in a joking way outside of the classroom). They asked her if she had told her students that "pot was the best thing in the world, and the best sex that you've ever had is while you're high." Mary *had* mentioned pot to her students; she had admitted to them that she had used it during college, but that she did not think it was a good thing to do. "I'd say 75 percent of those students were using, and I felt like I should give them some kind of feedback on it." The administrators asked her if she "used dope regularly"; she said she did not. The next question involved Mary's personal life.

> They said that I described my first sexual experience in detail, which I never did—I don't even know where that one came from. That I talk about my sexual life with my lesbian partner—they didn't say that, they just said my sexual life presently. I said, "No, I do not; I think that's a private thing that I don't share with anybody."

Mary was also accused of "playing favorites" with her students and sending special Christmas cards to two of the girls in her class.

> I said I had written a holiday card to every single student that I had in every class. It took me three days because I wrote a little personal note to each one. And they said, "Well, weren't they special to those two girls?" I said, "No, I bought a box of twenty-five cards and filled them all out. Nobody got a different card from anyone else."

Finally, the administrators accused Mary of "putting religion down" in her classroom.

> Then it began to dawn on me. I could sort of tell which students had been interviewed, and four of them come from very strong born-again Christian households. One of them has a father who's a preacher.

One was also the girl who had expressed her concern to Mary back in December.

Mary responded to each of the five areas. At the end of the meeting, she was asked if she had anything to say.

> I said I wanted to make known that I had been given the roughest group of kids and they had such a history that any teacher could document what those kids had put teachers through. I hadn't had any warning or help with this and I took it as a challenge and turned it around. The other thing I

wanted to say was that the school was extremely homophobic, that the bottom line here is that I'm an out, open lesbian, and you don't like it and some of the parents don't like it because of their religious beliefs, but I don't lie. The kids asked me and I told them, and people don't like that. They really don't want that kind of thing out there.

The superintendent told Mary he would write up the report and send it to the state Department of Education. He told her she could expect to hear from the state in about two weeks. By the middle of the summer, Mary was still waiting for her letter. She has hired a lawyer, who predicts that the superintendent may eventually back down, since state education laws provide for "progressive discipline," and Mary has never been observed. Meanwhile, though, she cannot apply for other jobs "because every other school district has a question on their application form that says, 'Are you currently under investigation?'" She will also be unable to teach summer school, a position that had been promised to her, and which she needs to help support her and her two school-age sons. As of summer, 1995, Mary was still waiting to hear from the state.

Mary's case is another chilling example of how powerful a few parents can be against an openly gay teacher. She lives in a state with a reputation for progressive politics, and with statewide legal protection for lesbians and gays. Forty-five miles from her town is one of the most diverse urban centers in the country. Yet within this conservative enclave, she is at the mercy of a few fundamentalists who want her out, and of an administration that refuses to stand up to them. Still, she says, there have been bright spots.

> A lot of my coworkers, teachers, people that I work with have called me and have been extremely supportive. The students that I have bumped into outside the campus at different Deaf events don't know what's going on. "Oh, when are you coming back? We miss you. We want you there." As a matter of fact, my students, the ones that were so difficult, attempted to petition to get me back, and it was confiscated by the principal.

Mary would like to take her school to court if she is not reinstated. Her union representative thinks she would stand a good chance of winning, because the administration would have to produce the names of her accusers and the dates and times of the supposed incidents. Yet given the structure of the court system, Mary's case could take two or three years. "In the meantime," she says, "I'm not viable for any kind of teaching job in this area. How do I support myself?" But no matter what happens, Mary doesn't plan to let the matter rest.

Even if they reinstate me, they haven't seen the end of it, because I'm not going to just sit back. I'm going to the papers, and I'm going to tell my story. I really want them to have some kind of workshop or something for the students, the parents, to get them to realize they're reacting out of this homophobia, and it's ridiculous. I don't know if that would ever happen, but I don't want to leave it like that. . . . What I really want right now is to get cleared so I can find other employment. Then I can pursue it safely.

Most important, Mary intends to stay in teaching, and she intends to remain there as an out lesbian.

I don't want them to have the power to take away something from me that I love and that I'm good at. They shouldn't have that right. . . . I will be out because it's really important to get these attitudes changed.

These stories show that discrimination based on sexual orientation is alive and well in the 1990s, and that gay teachers need and deserve civil rights protection as urgently as any other minority. Listening to them, it may seem that things have not come very far from the days when gay people were automatically branded criminal or insane, and a gay teacher would no more think of coming out of the closet than he would declare himself a convicted criminal.

Yet teachers who have been around for a while remind us that some things *have* changed, for lesbians and gays in general, and for gay teachers in particular. Pat Tomaso lived through the bar raids of the pre-Stonewall era, and remembers what it was like for gay teachers in those days.

I was in bars a couple of times when the police came, but they didn't take everybody. In those days, that's what they could do. They could just find one person, one excuse, one person under age, for example. . . . There used to be an ordinance that you could only have so many articles of the opposite sex clothing on. So one thing the police would do, is, they would check which way your shirt buttoned, if you had guys' pants on. . . . You're in a bar, you're having a good time, and all of a sudden the door opens, and then you turn and you look, and then there's another officer going to the back door to block any exit, and you're trapped. . . . They would call for the paddy wagon and everyone would be taken out of the bar, regardless. . . . And then they printed the names of people in the paper.

Pat remembers one historic evening when the police raided a popular Chicago gay bar.

I was in college at the time, and I can remember there was this little buzz going on very quietly around the cafeteria. . . . What had happened was a lot of doctors and a lot of teachers and a lot of lawyers, professional people, got arrested, and all their names were in the paper, and some of them were friends of our professors at school. From that day forward, there was work done to change that law so that no longer could they indiscriminately print everybody's name in the paper.

Pat's recollection of gay bars in the 1960s describes life in most big cities, where gays and lesbians sought each other's company in spite of police harassment. All that changed on the night of June 27, 1969, when a routine police raid on a gay bar in Greenwich Village erupted into a week of rioting that eventually led to the modern gay rights movement. Among the drag queens, militant activists, and ordinary gay and lesbian patrons at the Stonewall that night was Rina, who was leading a fairly satisfying life as a mostly out, prekindergarten teacher in Harlem.

Prior to Stonewall we used to go there just to dance. And when the police came to the door, there was a little buzzer under the [bar] and [the bartender] could ring the buzzer and everybody would switch partners. . . . Then one night we were told that they thought there was going to be a raid, and if you were in a profession or something . . . cross the street and go on to the other side.

Rina walked across the street to the small park at Sheridan Square, where she watched what happened next.

I stood by the gate of the park and all of a sudden the cops came, and I remember somebody had thrown something or done something. . . . The cops came in and they started to arrest people. I got very frightened and I ran away because I am not a very violent person and the violence was incredible. The nightsticks were flying. . . . It was angry. And we hadn't felt that anger for so long. I don't remember ever feeling that anger, and I didn't know where it was coming from.

Up to that time, Rina says, she had lived a fairly protected existence, even as a gay teacher. The next day, her principal warned her to stay away from the action for the rest of the week. "At that point in the New York City school system, though they were accepting us as gay people, they didn't want us to be put on the television." A few of her friends who had also been at the Stonewall were arrested and released; the more "militant" were held for a longer period of time. "And that was it. And it died down."

It would take years for the events that began with Stonewall to evolve into a political movement of visible gay activism, and even longer for lesbian and gay teachers to become visible in that activism. Today, in small towns and big cities, in rural farming communities and suburban bedroom communities, gay teachers are moving out of the closet and staging their own Stonewall Rebellion. As they do, they are finding themselves under a growing attack by those who would reverse the momentum of the past twenty-five years. Gay teachers have been the most visible targets in every one of these campaigns. They have also been on the front lines of the struggle.

9

Teaching Under Siege

DURING THE PAST DECADE, PROMOTERS OF "CITIZEN INITIA-tives" have mounted anti-gay campaigns in dozens of states and municipalities. In four states, Colorado, Oregon, Idaho, and Maine, these referendum questions have reached the ballot. Elsewhere, similar initiatives have failed to gather enough signatures or succumbed to legal challenges, but not without stirring up public sentiment against lesbians and gay men.

Voting "yes" on these questions generally means voting to deny the right of gay people to be protected from discrimination in housing, employment, public accommodation, and credit. Proponents draw their backing from conservative political organizations and right-wing fundamentalist groups like the Christian Coalition and Colorado's Focus on the Family. They base their arguments on the religious condemnation of homosexuality as sinful, and on the claim that there is a "gay agenda," concocted by homosexuals and their supporters, to take over the country.

Lesbian and gay teachers are prime targets for referendum proponents. Some ballot questions include language explicitly declaring homosexuality "unnatural," and making it illegal to present lesbian and gay people as "normal" within the public schools. In Colorado, Amendment Two included school districts in the list of agencies prohibited from protecting employees from discrimination based on sexual orientation. Oregon's failed 1992 Measure Nine would have gone further; in addition to denying civil rights protection, it would have mandated that state and local governments, "including specifically the State Department of Higher Education and the public schools," recognize "homosexuality, pedophilia, sadism, and masochism as abnormal, wrong, unnatural, and perverse." Measure Nine would also have required schools to teach that "these behaviors are to be discouraged and avoided." Two years later, the question reappeared as Ballot Measure Thirteen, the Minority Status and Child Protection Act; if approved at that time, it would have prevented "children, students, and employees" from being "advised, instructed, or taught . . . that homosexuality is the legal or social equivalent of race, color, religion, gender, age, or national origin," and would have barred public funds from being "expended in a manner that has the purpose or effect of promoting or expressing approval of homosexuality."

Idaho's Proposition One, defeated by voters in 1994, proposed to ban civil rights protection for lesbians and gays, mandating that "elementary and secondary school educators shall not discuss homosexuality as acceptable behavior" and "limiting adults access to library materials which address homosexuality." Maine's 1995 Question One was more subtle: it proposed to limit the Maine Human Rights Law to "race, color, sex, physical or mental disability, religion, age, ancestry, national origin, familial status, and marital status," effectively eliminating lesbians and gay men from future civil rights protection in the state. Question One would also have invalidated Portland's Human Rights Ordinance and repealed existing contract language protecting Portland's public school teachers from discrimination based on sexual orientation. It was defeated by a vote of 53 to 47 percent.

During these years, voters in several cities have also been asked to decide whether lesbian and gay citizens should be protected from discrimination. In 1992, voters in Portland, Maine, upheld a city council ordinance prohibiting discrimination based on sexual orientation; the following year, voters in Cincinnati overturned a similar ordinance, but the vote was subsequently struck down by a district court judge. Two years later, the Cincinnati City Council voted to repeal the original Human Rights Ordinance, effectively removing protection based on sexual orientation from the city's laws. And in Tampa, Florida, a 1995 initiative that would have repealed the city's gay rights ordinance was dismissed by a circuit judge, while voters in West Palm Beach defeated a ballot measure that would have repealed their city's gay rights law.

Lesbian and gay teachers have been in the spotlight during all these campaigns. If they are implicitly or explicitly out, they become obvious targets for antigay rhetoric about pedophilia and "special rights." If they are relatively closeted, they are forced to listen silently to hostile remarks from some of their students and colleagues. And, in the climate of hate that referendum campaigns create, their fears of exposure often escalate to terror. Many feel like Julie, who was teaching in Colorado Springs during the Amendment Two campaign.

> That's all you heard about. No matter when you turned the TV on, this was on. I felt like I was in an aquarium, out in the middle of the street, and everybody was pointing, "there's one, there's one."

Teachers who are open about their identity feel equally frightened. Barb remembers Measure Nine as "a grueling personal experience. Emotionally, it was just horrendous." As the campaign escalated, she felt less and less safe. "If I had my No on Nine button, which I did always, sometimes I'd think twice about it, about where I was."

Karen Cosper, another Oregon teacher who worked against Measure Nine, agrees, though she draws a distinction between the relatively progressive climate in her home city of Portland, where Ballot Measure Nine failed easily, and the increased jeopardy she still feels in other areas of the state.

> You know, it's easy to live in the city, in Multnomah County, where it was defeated three to one or something. But to realize once you cross the city line . . . That actually has stayed with me. I used to enjoy taking drives out in the country, or camping out, and I really am not comfortable leaving my city right now, still.

Whether they are closeted or openly gay, teachers feel personally attacked by referendum initiatives. Martha, a Portland middle school teacher, remembers an interview published in the Portland *Oregonian* in 1992.

> In this high school kid's opinion, he thought I shouldn't exist. . . . He didn't know me, I didn't know him. And yet he felt he could judge me.

Colorado teachers say their relationships with straight colleagues grew increasingly strained during Amendment Two. Michelle Serries remembers walking into the teachers lounge in the midst of a discussion about the issue.

> One guy was saying, "Oh, I think it's right. I think these people should be taken out and shot, and blah, blah, blah." And I turned around and I said, "You know, you work with one. You want to take me out and shoot me?" And they got real quiet. I said, "Thank you very much," and walked out.

Closeted teachers like Barbara and Shirley describe their life during Amendment Two as a double existence.

> We were working with EPOC [Equal Protection Colorado, the umbrella organization opposing the referendum], and sometimes we'd do that until

nine or ten, and then go to school the next day and have to face these kids, and teachers too. The hardest part of it was teachers . . . people who should know better.

Keith, a Colorado Springs high school teacher, worries about the plight of gay students during antigay political campaigns. "When I started in 1980," he recalls, "I had a student who was . . . almost openly gay, and she didn't care who knew about it. . . . It was sort of accepted. I don't think any of them ever were hassled about it." With the campaign, Keith says, the atmosphere "became more and more negative." Since then, gay students in Colorado are much more likely to be afraid, and "much less apt to be open."

As the rhetoric escalates, so does the harassment. Ron recalls:

On lunch duty one day I had on my No on Nine button, and . . . one kid leaned back and looked at my button and said, "So you're No on Nine?" And I said, "I'm No on Nine." He said, "Why are you No on Nine?" And I said, "Because I think it's discriminatory, and I think it's hurtful to people. I think it's really bad for our society." And then he says, "Well, are you a fag?" . . . I was just totally off guard. He didn't say, "Are you gay?" but, "Are you a fag?"

Curt entered his Colorado Springs classroom one day just as a group of students were discussing the campaign.

The kids didn't know I was gay, but what was coming out of their mouths was pure hate. . . . One was a football player. He was like 6′4″, huge kid. . . . He was saying things like "concentration camps" and "executing," and things like that. In the same breath he was talking about queers and fags. . . . Some other kids were arguing on the other side, of course, but he drowned them out. Although it wasn't directed at me per se, I still felt the venom.

Barbara heard the same rhetoric from her students.

I had one kid say, "Well, faggots should all be hanged." A lot of, "I don't want to have to work with anybody that's gay." And most of them said that they did not know anyone who was a gay person. . . . I tried very hard to remember that they weren't the ones who were speaking. It was their parents. It was the community. . . . They were just parroting everything that they heard from everybody else.

As a high school social studies teacher, Leslie frequently holds classroom discussions about current events. During the Amendment Two campaign, she was shocked to discover how thoroughly her students had absorbed the antigay rhetoric of Amendment proponents.

I said, "Let me put it this way. If a gay person worked down here at Safeway and . . . their employer says, 'Well, I don't like gay people, I'm firing you,' that would be blatant discrimination and that employee . . . would be able to say, 'That's illegal in the city and county of Denver.' If that person worked in the Safeway in Golden and the same thing happened, they would have no legal redress because Colorado allows people to be discriminated against on the basis of sexual orientation. . . . In forty-two out of fifty states, you can be evicted because you are gay—for that reason alone."

Leslie's students began to argue with her.

"That's not true, Miss Lane." "Well, you know, like I mean, like Amendment Two, and all that stuff, that's not true." And suddenly I just went, Jesus Christ. How is it that these kids have come to believe that gay people can live and work anywhere that they want and move freely in this country and not be discriminated against? I thought, God, what a good job the religious right has done. They've got these people believing . . . that we can do whatever the hell we want to do and now we want something more.

In Maine, Oregon, and Idaho, voters eventually rejected antigay ballot initiatives. In Colorado, however, Amendment Two passed by a margin of 53 to 47 percent.[1] Gay teachers now had evidence that a majority of their fellow-citizens agreed with the religious fundamentalists who said they had no right to be teaching children. For many, the knowledge was devastating.

"I was an emotional wreck," recalls Tracy Phariss. "It was just overwhelming. . . . I got telephone calls all that night. . . . I went through all of Kübler-Ross' [stages of grieving] for death. . . . I was angry, and then I was scared—I went through them all."

Gwen arrived at school the next day in disbelief. "Women were so moved they were crying at work, you know, lesbian women. They were [saying] 'I can't believe that this is what they think of me.' . . . [Teachers] most definitely feel more vulnerable."

Lyn Boudreau remembers watching the election results at a local gay restaurant with her partner, Betty Lynn.

We had a big fight when we got home. I was just devastated, and the fight was mainly about—I don't even know what it was about. It wasn't about

[1] Amendment Two has been declared unconstitutional by the Colorado Supreme Court. It is currently on appeal and will be decided by the U.S. Supreme Court in 1996.

anything real, it was just our emotions coming out. The next day . . . I went back to work numb. Just numb.

Leslie, too, remembers feeling "numb" the day after the election, "like when something happens to you that's really, really awful, and you just go through the motions of the day." During her planning period, a student teacher came into Leslie's room, a young man whom she liked, and to whom she was tacitly out.

He walks up to me and he turns around and he says, "I'm so sorry." And I just lost it. . . . He put his arms around me and he just hugged me for a long time, and I just cried.

Leslie has lived in Denver for over twenty years. Amendment Two was a profound attack not only on her sense of herself as a teacher, but on her feeling of being at home in the world.

I came here escaping the south, escaping this redneck little city. I came to Colorado. . . . I saw more mixed people like Brown and White and Black walking together down the street. . . . People were pretty much live and let live, and then it was like all of that was ripped away from me. My idea, you know—my place where I came and found myself.

The victory of antigay forces made Colorado's gay teachers fear for their jobs, and in some cases their lives. Not long after the beginning of the campaign, rumors began to fly about the opposition's secret tactics against teachers. Most common was the suspicion that Focus on the Family was compiling lists of gay and lesbian educators.

Bill was in a good place to assess the reliability of the rumor because of his position as a school administrator.

I called some friends in the administration to say, "Have you heard this rumor, and is it true?" and the denial of it was so blatant that it almost felt like, yeah, there was some truth to what was going on.

Curt heard about the witch-hunts at a meeting in Colorado Springs.

The rumor was that . . . they were going out of their way to find out who the unmarried teachers over thirty were, both male and female, and they were going to target them.

Back in more liberal Denver, Tim Brown recalls that representatives of Coloradans for Family Values "were calling school buildings and asking secretaries for the names and addresses of all single teachers. When they called

Denver, the secretary at the administration building said, 'I can't give you that information,' and hung up. But in Colorado Springs, they actually did give out names and addresses."

Whatever the extent of the witch-hunt, it appears to have backfired. Keith, who works with a Colorado Springs group called Citizen's Project, says that when his organization confronted Focus on the Family with allegations that they had been collecting names of gay teachers, "they denied it, and there was never any proof that they'd done it. . . . When it was reported there was a such a negative reaction that I think . . . whoever it was stopped."

The effect of the rumors on gay teachers is not hard to imagine. For a closeted teacher like Julie, who had just joined a gay teachers group in Colorado Springs, fear merged into paranoia.

> When I went to the potluck, the teachers group, I felt like Focus on the Family were sitting in cars with binoculars, writing down license plates. I was really afraid to do anything. I told my therapist, "Are they sitting out there writing down license plate numbers and trying to find out where you live?"

Given the rise in the number of hate crimes during antigay political campaigns, the increase in casual bigotry expressed by many straight students and teachers, and the much-publicized murder of a gay man and a lesbian in Salem, Oregon, during the 1992 campaign, Julie's fears may not be paranoia after all. The fact that she is still teaching in her Colorado Springs high school, and still attending meetings of the teachers group, is a tribute to her courage.

Washington State is one of the places where attempts to stage an antigay referendum have not yet succeeded, largely due to the efforts of a statewide civil rights coalition called Hands Off Washington. Ruth Frobe and her friends realize that if the question reaches the ballot, they will face the same risks and challenges that gay teachers have endured in Colorado, Oregon, Idaho, and Maine. So far, their activism has been limited to wearing T-shirts and donating money. Frank says he taped a HOW bumper sticker to the back window of his car and displayed it, "except for Monday through Friday between seven and four o'clock. . . . I'd take it off as I'd go to school. I just wasn't ready for that."

But these Washington teachers know that they will probably not be able to stay on the sidelines forever. D. J. Reed says:

> I used to feel like it didn't matter, because there were gay people, or gay friendly people in charge somewhere that would make bad things not

happen, and so I didn't have to be politically involved. And I don't believe it anymore. I really feel like if I don't speak out, and if people like me don't speak out, then we're all gonna get screwed or beat up, or killed, or fired. The older I get, the more I risk by speaking out. But the more—you know, I have to.

Reaching Out

"There was a time when I was going to make the revolution, and there were only ten people in it. I'm glad I got to a different place."

Jan Goodman, *elementary school principal, California*

10

Families

As they balance the complicated risks and challenges of their lives, gay teachers find their greatest reassurance in the knowledge that they are not alone. Some turn to their families, or build "families of choice" with partners and friends. Others find their deepest affirmation in spiritual or religious affiliations. Many have begun coming together with other gay educators to form local and national organizations. And all are discovering the importance of heterosexual allies in schools and communities. Whatever their primary support, gay teachers are learning that no matter how difficult or frightening their situation, they can feel stronger and prouder when they join together with others.

Teachers lucky enough to enjoy close relationships with their birth families find parents and siblings the most immediate source of comfort. Sometimes, parents are more accepting than their children expect them to be. Ruth waited until she was settled in a teaching position and a relationship before telling her father that she was gay.

I'll never forget it, he said, "Well, I have never seen you so happy [as] in the last year." And I got off the phone and I just bawled, because all these years, I had done fantasies in my head: "Well, I never want to see you again," and "You're out of my will," and "Don't ever come by my house again," 'cause I've heard horror stories like that and I feared the worst.

Martha received an equally positive message from her father.

I was twenty-three when I fell in love with a woman, and that was wonderful. I came out to my father—my mother had died the year before—and he was very sweet. He said he could see how somebody would be in love with me. Isn't that nice?

Some gay teachers find inspiration, as well as support, from their parents. Michael Scott grew up in a small town in Idaho, where his family owned a series of restaurants. Today, he is a union activist and a veteran of the 1992 and 1994 Oregon ballot campaigns. Mike attributes his courage and his social conscience to the values he learned from his family, especially his mother.

She would hire who she thought was best for the job and treat them with the respect that they deserved, didn't matter who they were . . . my sister . . . had a couple of friends who were Mexican American and she'd bring them home. Mom treated them with the utmost respect as she did anybody, and I think I saw that and took a lesson from her.

Dan Dromm says working with his mother gave him his first experience as a White teacher in a community of color.

My mother was a day-care center director, and I don't think she's got a prejudiced bone in her body. . . . I used to work with her in the day-care centers when I was a teenager. . . . Matter of fact . . . I was assistant director of a day-care center in the center of Harlem for almost seven years. And I really believe that it was there that I learned my community organizing. If I'm good at it, at all, that's where I learned it.

Dan's mother has also showed him the meaning of loyalty. His two brothers have not spoken to him for eighteen years, and did not even invite him to their weddings. "It's really divided the family," he says. "But my mother has always stood by me."

Some parents who are initially distressed to learn that they have a gay child later become part of their son or daughter's support system. Dave Larson's parents are devout Catholics and prominent members of their rural Wisconsin church. Dave came out to them just as he was preparing to enter his first teaching job, and anticipated the worst: "I told them in March, and I kind of made plans for where I was gonna spend Thanksgiving and Christmas the next year." But after the initial shock, Dave's parents responded better than he could have hoped.

Originally they were too shaken up to talk to me. They were very concerned that they'd say something really damaging, because they were so emotional. . . . This summer . . . I'd just gotten my first job and it pays really,

really well for a first-year teacher. When I was staying at home, my parents saw that I was really happy and comfortable and that I seemed my normal self or even better than my normal self, and that helped them a lot to adjust.

Linda's parents have taken a long time to accept her lesbian identity. She says that during the year when she was forced to resign from her junior high position, she was "pretty estranged" from her family; her mother "still doesn't want to know that any of that happened." But by now, Linda says, she has "worked things through," and likes the fact that her family are "wonderful solid community citizens that everybody knows and likes." Students in Linda's high school, which is located in the community where her family has lived for generations, "love hearing about my grandmother. She's quite a character. . . . I feel comfortable with that, since it's a part of who I am."

Sometimes, another adult relative can play a supportive role in a gay teacher's life. For Jan Goodman, it was her grandfather.

[He] always believed that if we're on earth, the world should be a better place because of us. . . . He was a socialist and he had an eighth-grade education, and he marched and he did all this really good stuff.

Jan says her grandfather's commitment to social justice showed her the way out of an unhappy childhood, and has influenced her work as a teacher-activist.

He never told me to do it, but [there] was this really strong sense that the world was not fair, that I had when I was a child that really made me numb for many years. For me acting on this unfair thing has really made me powerful.

Gary remembers a favorite uncle, the only member of his family to ask him about Vietnam.

My parents never asked. My sisters never asked. My aunts and uncles never asked. My friends never asked. Nobody ever asked. . . . We had been in some lake and my uncle asked me how it was. We were just floating on inner tubes, and we sat and floated for an hour and a half while I talked about it for the first time.

Three months later, Gary's uncle died, and he became deeply depressed. Part of the depression came from the war experiences he had never fully come to terms with; part from his grief over the loss of his uncle, the only one who had ever asked; and part from his conflicted emotions over being a gay teacher. Eventually, Gary was able to sort through his emotions (he says he still goes back to his therapist "for yearly checkups"), with the support of a gay teachers group in Colorado Springs, where he is "the keeper of the list" of members' names and addresses.

Teachers with gay siblings or relatives find this shared bond an important source of support. Rina's first gay role model was a cousin whom she met before she had even come out to herself.

> He took me around to all the gay places in the city. He was about three years older than I was, and introduced me to the gay world when I was about fourteen. And I was very, very impressed.

Doralynn says her coming out has "paved the way" for her lesbian younger sister. "We relate," she says. "So it's easier than many."

Sue and her brother came out to each other just as he was starting to cope with AIDS. The relationship that developed between them helped her come out to her parents, and sustained her as she struggled to honor his memory during the uproar over the AIDS Quilt at her Oregon middle school.

For Rebecca, accepting her older sister's lesbian identity was part of the process of accepting her own identity.

> There was a point that I was dealing with my own homophobia against her, against gays and lesbians, and it took me a long time to realize what was going on. I think I really needed to do a lot of maturing and growing.

Rebecca's acceptance of her sister helped her to develop the values of tolerance she now tries to pass on to her students.

> Her friends were so unique and genuine, so it caused me to put down some barriers and open up to see myself. Once I did that, I could look inward. . . . I realized that people are who they are . . . wonderful and fascinating.

Occasionally, support comes from straight ex-spouses, who are able to help their former partners start new lives, and even new teaching careers. Shirley expected the worst when she told her husband that she had fallen in love with a woman, but his response was surprisingly understanding. "He said that it was not anything he could fight. If it was another man, he could fight it. If it was another woman, he couldn't." When Shirley moved from Indiana to Colorado Springs, where her partner was already teaching, her husband (soon to be her ex-husband), came with her and helped her "get car registrations and all the things you have to do when you first move to a new state."

Christy says her husband is still a good friend. "We have a wonderful relationship. We still live together, kind of co-share the house." As her children grow older, Christy expects to move out on her own, or move in with her partner, but for the time being, her husband's support makes life as a closeted teacher easier to bear.

But not all gay teachers find such ready support in their families. Julie Anderson, a high school librarian in Kent, Washington, says she left her home state of Kansas "to get away from Bob Dole and other people like him."

> My parents are God-fearing Republicans. I haven't spoken to them now for about five or six years. They moved to Colorado, and I'm pretty sure they voted for Amendment Two. I finally had to say to them, "Go away. You're driving me crazy." They'd send me multiple-page, typed, xeroxed letters. . . . "Come home, let us help you. See if we can reverse this slide into horrible events."

Julie's father happens to be a retired school administrator. "For a while, when I was still communicating with him, I wouldn't tell him I was applying for a job because I was afraid he was going to call and say, 'Hey, do you know this person's gay?'"

Frank's father was a teacher and school principal who did not talk to Frank or his lesbian sister during the last six months of his life. "He was a very, very prejudiced man, and if he was actually alive today . . . he would be the one sitting there going, 'That dyke teacher.'"

Rebecca describes her mother as "very homophobic," and has never told her about the student harassment she suffered at school.

> If my mom knew this stuff was happening with me, she would be out of her mind. . . . I went to visit her in Florida on April vacation and I had this novel that I was going to take down to the beach and read, and she grabbed it and said, "Oh, don't take this down there. Somebody might see what you are reading."

Alejandra Dubove's parents have never visited her in Boston, though she occasionally goes home to Texas to see them. "Our conversations are very surface," she says. "About my car, the weather, my oil changes, and how's the car battery." For support, Alejandra turns to her partner's parents, who welcome her as a member of their family, and to GLSTN, the national Gay, Lesbian, and Straight Teachers Network, which she joined a year ago.

> Before that I had a lot of support from friends. I think with a lot of gay people, their friends become their family. It certainly was [true] for me. . . .

And the straight friends I have, obviously they couldn't be my friends if they weren't accepting and supportive, so that's very helpful.

Other gay teachers have found support in P-FLAG, (Parents, Families, and Friends of Lesbians and Gays), an international organization whose members serve as advocates for their lesbian and gay relatives and friends. Christy started going to P-FLAG meetings after she came out to her parents and they refused to talk to her. She says P-FLAG "has been wonderfully supportive—I just come back feeling so good. . . . It even gave me the strength to send down to my mom some books that they have recommended. So I'm even getting some support from her."

At forty-two, Rick is still not out to his family:

They're about eight hundred miles away, and every time I come to grips with saying, "This is the visit that I'm going to tell them," it's so different back there that I don't. . . . I can just see my mother going to church and people saying, "Oh, did you hear about Evelyn's son?" And yet, I have real guilt feelings that they don't know me, and I've distanced myself from my family.

Meanwhile, Rick has found "a lot of Colorado moms" in the local P-FLAG chapter, where he is on the Board of Directors. He says they partly make up for the family back in Iowa that hopes he can someday come out to.

For gay teachers who are forced to conceal their identity in school, the most important support comes from friends with whom they do not have to hide. Annette and her partner send their daughter to an independent school where they are completely open and completely accepted.

From the get-go we came out as a gay and lesbian family in our application. . . . They accepted us knowing what we were about, and it's just felt so good to be out with her friends' parents, and the teachers and the community at large there. I'm glad I have that in my life to counter all the hostility.

Christy and her partner "Sue," who teach at the same special needs school on Long Island, have "some really wonderful friends" who support them in their struggles to survive their closeted lives as teachers. Christy volunteers at the Gay and Lesbian Switchboard, and finds her work there important to her own self-understanding. "Every time I have to take a call from someone who's struggling, it gives me a chance to kind of dig in there and figure out my place."

Gay men and lesbians who are parents say their children play a special role in their lives as teachers. Karen came out when her daughter, "Judy," was seven and her son was nine. Initially, Judy was "real homophobic. . . . It was like, 'I wish you weren't a lesbian, Mom.'" But during Karen's battle with the parents who tried to have her fired, Judy became her mother's strongest advocate.

> She was valedictorian, so she gave the "V" address. It was about discussing differences, and she said the word "homosexual" at least four times. People came up to her and said, "'Thank you, Judy, that needed to be said." . . . It brought tears to my eyes.

Karen says her son "has never had a problem" with her sexual orientation, probably because his best friend's mother in their former hometown was also a lesbian. "Cindy [Karen's partner] is his other mom and she is to Judy also. . . . I can't imagine if I had a bad relationship what this would have been like."

Christy's children, like Karen's, "had some struggles" when their mother came out, but are now more supportive. She says that the message she gets from them is, "We're uncomfortable about this, Mom, it's really different, but we see how happy you are." Most important to Christy, her children treat Sue "like a significant other, and that feels real supportive."

Support from his adolescent daughter was an important motivation for Allan Arnaboldi, a Massachusetts elementary school teacher, to march in the local Gay Pride march with Gay and Lesbian Educators, a local teachers group.

> I came out to her when she was twelve. I told her that I wanted to march in this Gay Pride march, but I needed to know how she felt about it, and if it was really a problem, I would not do it. . . . I checked in with her a day or so before the march . . . and things were fine. I didn't march with a mask or anything. I thought about it and decided to just be myself.

Like Karen, Allan was happy to discover that his daughter had a friend from a gay family.

> When my daughter got to high school, she developed this really close friendship with her friend, Linda, and one day she just kind of said to Linda, "You know, my father's gay." And Linda said, "Did you know my mother's a lesbian?"

Kevin Gogin sees his role as Director of Support Services for Gay and Lesbian Youth in the San Francisco schools through the lens of his identity as a gay parent. In fact, he says, one of the reasons he accepted the job was his concern for the world his daughter "Rachel" will inhabit. As an example of some of the attitudes he is working to change, Kevin describes an experience during the 1993 March on Washington.

> There was this one group sitting on the side, and they'd say, you know, "Go to hell." Rachel asked, "They don't like us." And she goes, "Why?" . . . Here's this four-year-old who I have to pick up because there's these people screaming that we should be killed.

Rodney's relationship with his daughter "Susan" was an important part of his coming out process, even though Susan continued to attend the Christian school where Rodney had formerly taught.

> She's a beautiful person, but she hasn't really come into her own yet as far as what she really believes about things. She struggles really strongly internally, I know, with the fact that her father whom she loves very much is gay. She's been taught all her life that gay people are bad, they're sinners, they're an abomination before God, and all these kinds of things.

Recently, Susan told her father about a seventeen-year-old friend who had committed suicide, apparently without reason. Some details of the story led Rodney to suspect that the boy might have been struggling with his sexual identity.

> I said, "Maybe he was coming to the realization that he was gay," and she said, "Yeah, maybe he was." She said, "I think you're right."

This conversation seemed to bring Rodney and his daughter closer together. She has told three of her best friends that her father is gay, and, to Rodney's delight, they have been very accepting.

Carolyn Wood has a close relationship with her son despite losing one of Oregon's first lesbian custody cases when "Martin" was eighteen months old. Throughout his childhood, Carolyn assumed he knew she was a lesbian, but at one point she felt she needed "to say the words. I took him on a run. He was probably ten. I told him that I was a lesbian, and he said, 'I know.' . . . So that was pretty sweet."

Over the years, Carolyn has had close ties with her son.

> He has virtually outed me every place that he's been, so there are no secrets at the school where I teach. . . . I coached his soccer team and was always

available. . . . When he was in high school I was really close and I timed the track meets, and all that kind of stuff. And then when he graduated I moved into his school.

Unlike Carolyn, Shirley and Barbara plan to wait for Shirley's children to leave high school before coming out in their respective schools. Shirley says:

I'd like to be much more open. But then it impacts the kids in their school. You know, if someone else knows who we are and what we are, then they go tell their kids that they can't go play with Sharon, they can't go to Sharon's house. . . . I think the time's getting really close. . . . My daughter's a senior.

Shirley's caution is compounded by the fact that Sharon has recently come out as a lesbian, and has had a hard time at school.

They shoved her around. They'd call her names. . . . I was really worried that she wasn't even going to finish school. . . . A lot of the gay kids will stay away from her now, because they're afraid if they hang around her then they'll get identified.

Jessie is another teacher who plans to be more "daring" about coming out after her children are grown and "won't have to take the flak for who I am." In the meantime, she says, she teaches them that "you love who you love, and it's okay to love whoever." Sounding as much like a teacher as a parent, she adds:

I say that we all have gifts and we're all different, and what God gives us we have to use, and that the only way to teach is to share the gifts we have. And that teaching people not to hate is a very special gift.

Lesbian and gay teachers who become coparents of their partner's children find family relationships as difficult and as rewarding as they are in any blended family. As adults whose lives are dedicated to young people, gay educators are especially sensitive to the responsibilities of parenting. Rina says:

When you make a commitment to a woman and her two children, it's not a commitment just to the woman, but a commitment to her kids. And I as a teacher was not going to mess up two kids' lives and say, "Oh, yes, I'm gonna commit myself," and then walk away.

For many, the pain of having to hide at work is intensified by the pain of not being known as a parent. Leslie longs for public acknowledgment of her relationship with her partner's daughter Emily, whom they have coparented since her infancy.

> I'm the person that got her involved in sports and soccer, which she's been playing since she was four. She ice skates. I got her involved in that. She plays softball, she plays tennis. I got her involved in all those things because for me movement was always so joyful. . . . But I don't have a name. There isn't anything that's legitimate, that just says it.

Even those who are relatively out often feel that a significant part of themselves is invisible. Carolyn Wood and her partner, Rose Bond, are both open about their sexual orientation at school, but Rose says:

> I can still be out to new people in the office, and I'll talk about, "Yeah, Martin's going back," and I see their eyebrows go up, like, "Well, who's Martin?" And then what do I say? "He's my boy"? "He's my son"? It's like this problem I have of what my name is. Or who I'm called in relation to him.

Rose wants to "be more out," not just for herself, but "for the family I've made." But she finds it hard to know exactly how. "Except just to stop editing and just talk about my family, talk about Martin, and say, 'Well, that's Carolyn's son, my boy.'"

Whatever the nature of their family constellation, gay teachers find meaning in those families, and strength that helps them endure the special difficulties of life as a lesbian or gay educator. Sometimes the support is open and available; sometimes, as Christy puts it, teachers do not have "a clump of support," but gather it in many different places. "Together," she says, "they all kind of help."

11

The Inner Voyage

IN THE LONG JOURNEY TO DEFINE THEMSELVES AS GAY teachers, educators turn inward as well as outward. For some, the inner voyage is a secular one of philosophical reflection or analysis. For others, the path is more spiritual. Some teachers find comfort in their earliest religious traditions, while others seek new spiritual meaning for their lives as lesbian and gay educators.

Cary is a gay teacher who has maintained his childhood faith throughout the turmoil of growing up and coming out. He attributes his religious faith to his grandfather, a deacon in the Southern Baptist church. Despite the limitations of growing up Southern Baptist ("you can't dance, you can't drink"), Cary says his family encouraged him "to have my own relationship with God apart from the church and what the church believed." Now, in adulthood, Cary still feels that relationship, "stronger than ever."

Like many lesbians and gay men, Cary has found spiritual meaning at the Metropolitan Community Church, a national denomination serving lesbian and gay Christians. In addition to his connection with the Baptist faith of his childhood, Cary writes curriculum for the Dallas MCC and attends services there once a week.

Torey is another native Texan raised Baptist who turns to the religious tradition of his childhood. In his case, the tradition was that of the Black Baptist church, where despite negative messages about homosexuality, Torey found the basis for a "very personal" relationship with God.

I just really came to the resolve at a very early age that God loves everybody. In my reading and in my own interpretation and understanding of my religion and what God is all about, God is love. No matter who you are or what you are.

During his college years, Torey was a deacon in the Baptist church on his campus, where he felt comfortable enough to come out to the campus ministers. More recently, he says his religious faith helped him to survive his traumatic first year of teaching. "I definitely would not have made it through this year had I not been very in touch with my spirituality," he says. "And I do get that from within the African American religious community."

Lyn Boudreau is one of many gay teachers who found their first vocation in religious life, and left only after coming out. "I've always been spiritual by nature, you know, in kind of a search all my life," she reflects, "and as a Catholic woman, that's kind of what you do."

After ten years as a nun, Lyn fell in love with another woman, and for the first time in her life, felt "right." At the same time, she says, she "carried a lot of guilt and shame. . . . I mean, talk about closets—a closet within a closet in the convent. You had to come out of the closet just to be in another closet."

Lyn left Catholicism, not because of "the liturgy per se or the teachings of the Catholic Church," but because of "the way it was played out politically." Her partner, Betty Lynn, was attending a Congregational Church in Colorado Springs when they met, and when Lyn accompanied her there, she found her spiritual home.

> Like many gay and lesbian Christians in America today, it is not a contradiction for me at all. I think there's a fallacy out there that people think if you're gay or lesbian that you can't be Christian. . . . But I don't find any contradiction that God made me this way, with this sexual orientation. It's kind of my basis of who I am.

Jean Bourg, who spent three years in a convent immediately after high school, says choosing religious life was "not uncommon" for young women of her generation (she is forty-six). "It was the quick and easy way out of Louisiana and out of family difficulties—meaning poverty." Jean now considers herself "totally recovered" from her Catholic upbringing, but has recently joined the Unitarian Church, because "they are very supportive of gays and lesbians."

Peter entered religious life partly to avoid acknowledging his homosexuality. Eventually, he realized he could not hide from his own identity, and left to become a parochial school teacher. The best thing that happened to him during his time in the religious order was his friendship with "Glen," a Brother who lived next door and who left a short time before Peter did. Soon after he left religious life, Peter visited Glen, and discovered that he had guessed the truth: Glen, too, was gay. Glen became "the brother I wish my own could have been," a mentor and friend. "He paid for my first therapy. He bought me my first suit for my first job interview." A few years later, Glen died of AIDS; in fact, it was Peter's desire to attend Glen's memorial service that precipitated the final break with his principal at the school he calls the "nuthouse." And, by a coincidence that Peter feels was more than coincidence, the day he received the phone call for his new job was exactly one year after Glen's death.

Bob Bradley, who spent a number of years in the seminary before coming out, wanted to be a priest "ever since eighth or ninth grade." When he first realized he was gay, he came out to his confessor, who suggested that Bob "leave the priesthood and get married—and that would cure me." Bob took the first part of the priest's advice, though not the second, and remains "a very devout Catholic, very involved." Within his church, Bob has been an advocate for acceptance of lesbians and gays.

> A pastor once said to me, what did I see my role as in the church? And I said, "To be a thorn in its ass. To really nudge it on." ... I am a Catholic who knows that God caused me to be who I am, in the fullness and totality of my nature, which includes my sexuality. I stand tall and proud as a gay person who is Roman Catholic. And no one can tell me otherwise.

Though at one time in his life Bob was involved with Dignity, the gay Catholic organization, he calls that "a transitional point."

> It was a time of coming to terms with being gay, when I first came out of the closet, immersed myself in everything gay. I would only go to gay plays, or gay bars, gay entertainment, gay restaurants, and gay religious services.

Today, however, Bob and his partner Luis attend a mainstream Catholic church in New York where women play a significant role in the worship services, and many of the parishioners are gay.

Teachers who have left religious life, or have felt rejected by conventional religious institutions, need to redefine their spirituality for themselves. Phil Robinson was raised in an environment where "we always felt like we were going to church and getting ready for Sunday church." Growing up as an African American boy in New York, he says, "religion was a stronghold." Now he sees things "not so much from a religious context but more of a spiritual context. ... One of my strongholds is a belief in a higher power ...

believing that there really is something that does guide me. . . . In the midst of the bad, there's always some good, as I see it."

As a teacher at a Christian school, Rodney's religious life was closely tied to his life as an educator. When he came out and left teaching, he abandoned many of the fundamentalist beliefs that he had shared with his colleagues.

> As far as God and I are concerned, I'm a Christian. But as far as the church and I are concerned, I'm not a Christian. And if it means that I can't be a gay person and be a Christian, I'll be a gay person, because I don't agree that that's true Christianity, when they're condemning other people.

Rodney declares that "the term Christian" doesn't mean much to him anymore; yet when he talks about a visit to the Metropolitan Community Church it is obvious that he is still wrestling with his fundamentalist past.

> I've gone, and it scares me. I just can't reconcile somebody standing up there in front and saying, "You are gay and God loves you the way you are," because all my life I've been taught that that can't be true. It just sends chills up and down my back and it depresses me.

Like Rodney, Rick has struggled with his identity as a Christian and his church's teachings about homosexuality—in his case, the Lutheran church of his small-town childhood.

> I think I have a real strong personal religion. I don't go to church every Sunday, but I've read the Bible twice, really have tried to examine some things in there, and still felt a lot of guilt that . . . I couldn't be gay and be a Christian, and yet on the other hand I was gay and I am Christian, so how do you separate them?

When Rick talked to the associate minister at his Colorado Springs church, he was "kind of politely told not to come back."

> Well, then, I did go speak to the head minister, and they do now have a support group for gay members. There's only six of us that go, but it has been nice.

Other gay teachers find spiritual support in liberal religious communities, or in lesbian and gay societies within traditional denominations. Alan Kelly-Hamm, whose life as a Quaker is a central part of his identity, says he feels "called to be a teacher, called to be gay, and called to be a Friend." Ruth met her partner at a Georgia chapter of Integrity, the lesbian and gay organization within the Episcopal church, and loves telling her colleagues at school, "Yes, I met my roommate at church." Allan Gold is active in a California lesbian and gay synagogue, and says that the spiritual community he finds there helps him cope with his partly closeted life as a school psychologist.

Some gay teachers are still searching for spiritual homes to take the place of the ones that no longer feel comfortable. Joseph misses his connection with Catholicism, and says regretfully that "in our family, it's either Catholicism or nothing." But he has also become friendly with a young woman who studies Buddhism and meditation, and says, "I just find religion in bird-watching or being out of doors."

Jessie grew up in an agnostic Italian family and "explored all kinds of spirituality" as a young woman. Lately, she has joined her local Presbyterian church, "which is very much into social activism." She enjoys the ritual and tries to "edit and teach from the Bible things that I think are important, and . . . point out things that are missing." Most of all, she feels the church connection is important for her two children, aged seven and nine. "I think kids need some tangible concept of goodness, and not something really abstract," she says.

Pat Tomaso, another "recovered" Catholic, takes issue with the church's stands on women and homosexuality. But, having attended a Catholic university and studied "metaphysics and all these other classes," she says she has come "to my own place and my own understanding." Her belief system now is based on "my higher powers and the grace of the universe, the goddesses, whatever. I prefer that."

Dave Larson no longer attends Catholic services, largely because of the Church's teaching about homosexuality. The final insult came when his parents consulted their priest about their son's sexual orientation.

> They talked to my priest, and told him that I was gay . . . and he said, "Well, he can still be a Catholic if he doesn't have sex." And my mom had the presence of mind to say, "Well, I really don't think that's what he wants." I felt really betrayed.

Dave misses the religious experience he used to find in church, and wishes he had "more of a spiritual center."

> I felt when I was going to church that I was part of problems that were greater than mine and it helped diminish whatever I was going through. But I also remember praying during Lent that I wouldn't be gay, and it didn't happen. So, you know, I have some frustrations from that too.

He has attended services at Dignity, and thinks he might go again, to "try to find a place" for himself. "I don't rule religion out, and I don't feel angry against the Church, but just a little disappointed."

Jeff was raised in a Protestant family, but converted to Catholicism during his adolescence, when he became involved in a youth group with some of his Catholic friends and met a "real fantastic pastor" at the local Catholic church. Although he is not explicitly out at his Catholic school, he finds the women he teaches with very progressive, and considers himself "a very liberal Catholic." He says hopefully, "I guess I'm . . . of the idea that everything goes through cycles, and everyone will eventually come around—maybe with another Pope."

For some teachers, spirituality infuses every part of life. Peggy, who is almost completely closeted in her work life, still finds teaching "a spiritual activity . . . totally integrated into the deepest places of me." She refers to herself as "a natural integrator," and says things must make sense for her "in a total, connected web." For this reason, hiding her identity at school is especially painful; at the same time, her spiritual life, and her connections with her church help her live with the paradoxes.

Larry, another gay educator who finds inspiration in his faith, describes his relationship with God from the perspective of a teacher living with HIV. But his words could apply to all those who feel a spiritual presence guiding them in their journey as gay teachers.

> My desire more than anything in the world to be a principal, my desire to finish my doctorate, those are the things that motivate me the most to be positive and stay alive. . . . I [believe] that I will always be here as long as He has something for me to do, and I'm taking advantage of that opportunity. I have no fear of death as long as I know that I'm doing what I'm supposed to be doing.

12

Coming Together

AS THEY REACH BEYOND THEIR IMMEDIATE FAMILIES, GAY teachers build networks in and out of school. Some of their most important affirmations come when they find each other.

Ruth Frobe and her friends have been each other's support group for a long time. Ruth, D. J. Reed, Sharon, and Jody went to college together; Frank and Wendy met them after they had all become teachers. In addition, Frank and Jody teach at the same junior high school and often look for each other during the day. Jody recalls:

> Frank came in on my birthday when I turned thirty, and he brought me flowers and kissed me in the gym. All the kids were . . . going crazy, because the rest of the time they're sitting around the locker room going "that dyke" and "that fag."

These friends say that knowing one another is what enables them to cope with life as gay teachers. "I could not live without the people in this room," says Jody, looking around at her friends. "I would just curl up and die. They're my family."

Not all gay teachers are lucky enough to find a circle with so much shared history, but most manage to identify supportive people in different parts of their lives. During her last year in graduate school, Michelle lived with two other lesbian student teachers.

> I remember a lot of jokes about how we had to get in drag, and, for some of the school systems, wear nylons and heels. We talked about various

responses to "Do you have a boyfriend?" You know, starting to face some of the issues of coming out even in our student teaching.

Since returning to graduate school for her doctoral degree, Peggy has built a network of trusted allies with whom she can be open about her sexuality.

My big job in the last year has been getting to the place where I now no longer move to any place in my life where there isn't someone who sees me whole. When I'm with my family, there's someone. When I'm in church, there's someone—she's the only one, but she's there. . . . At the university there are lots of people.

Finding other gay teachers in their own schools makes a significant difference for those who are still closeted. When Michelle began teaching high school, she had just arrived in the Bay Area and knew no one.

There was a reception at the beginning of the year and someone that I had met there introduced me to a bunch of the other lesbians on campus, so I got to know who they all were. But even from day one I was warned that the school was very homophobic and that there was a very strong fundamentalist Christian community both at the school and in the town. . . . So my friend and I were very careful all year to stay very closeted.

Knowing other gay teachers helped Michelle survive her first year as a closeted teacher, though her hiding strategies worked so well that one gay colleague did not even guess he was working with a lesbian. "He told me after we both came out to each other that he thought I was a straight young Christian virgin. I said, 'Guess again, buddy.'"

In recent years, informal networks of gay teachers have grown up around the country. Some provide a comfortable place for lesbian and gay teachers in the same community to socialize in a safe environment, while others are more political. The gay teachers group in Colorado Springs is mostly a social organization, though many of its members became politically active during the Amendment Two campaign. Unlike most teachers groups, it includes educators from college and university campuses as well as elementary and secondary schools.

For Curt, this group is a welcome alternative to the bar scene, which he finds very "artificial." ("I'm not in my twenties anymore, or teens, or even my thirties," he explains.) John C. Miller, a faculty member at the University of

Colorado/Colorado Springs, and one of the founders of the Colorado Springs network, says the group helps gay teachers find other support services and find each other.

> I've been at so many occasions when people would say, "You know, I wanted to ask you about coming to this meeting, but I was afraid to do it." People who work in the same schools, same districts, have been able to sense an environment where they can find support.

Gary discovered the group through Colorado College geology professor Bruce Loeffler, a founding member and an out gay activist during Amendment Two. He says joining the teachers group was "my biggest coming out."

> Nobody had ever invited me to a private party. I didn't know anybody. I've been here sixteen years, I knew Bruce thirty seconds, and he said, "Oh, you should come to this group."

For Julie, who was out to "maybe three people" before attending her first teachers group meeting, finding other gay teachers was frightening, but also very liberating. "The neat thing was that I wasn't in the house two minutes when I ran into a fellow that I teach with who [is] gay, and that gave me someone to talk to."

Michelle Serries is a longtime member of the Denver teachers group, an association of lesbian and gay educators that played a more political role than its Colorado Springs counterpart during the 1992 campaign. Michelle says many teachers find it reassuring just to know the group exists.

> I get a lot of calls from teachers who, even if they don't come, seem to be very glad that there is something out there. . . . They want to know that there are other teachers, and that there's a place you can go and just be in a room full of people that are as dedicated to education as you feel, and also have the commonality of being gay and lesbian.

Gay teachers groups, whether social or political, formal or informal, make it possible to take risks that would otherwise be unthinkable. Allan Arnaboldi is one of the founders of GALE, the Gay and Lesbian Educators group of western Massachusetts, which grew out of Professor Pat Griffin's research project on gay teachers.

> I'd gone through all this empowerment stuff beforehand, and I knew each step made me feel more powerful. . . . I'm really glad that I had GALE [to] help me get to where I am.

Martha was an early member of CUE, the Cascade Union of Educators, a mostly social gay teachers group in Portland, Oregon.

> I realized at the time there was a part of me that thought, well, maybe it's not okay to be a lesbian and to be a teacher. And . . . when I got in the group it was more like, Oh, I don't have to hold my breath anymore. . . . Just to know other fine teachers made me realize that it was okay, it was good.

Back on the East Coast, Rebecca has been involved in an informal support group that draws its membership from southern Maine and northern New Hampshire.

> A professor from UNH [the University of New Hampshire] . . . put it together. You meet somebody who is a biology teacher there, you meet somebody else who is a music teacher here, and all of a sudden there are people. I remember the day that all of this happened—the cup and the calendar—and going to our support group and telling them. You could have heard a pin drop in that room. [And] afterward, to be so supportive and come up to you and give you a hug and say, what a big step you are taking, and that kind of stuff. Very supportive.

Dave Larson admits he was "a little nervous" before attending the first meeting of a Chicago-area teachers group, but adds that "the fear of those kind of situations gets less and less every time for me. . . . I'm glad I went." At the group's second or third meeting, organizers asked how many people would be willing to march in the local Gay Pride parade. "They wanted a show of hands . . . because there's no point in getting the banner if there's only gonna be three people behind the banner. Our hands shot up."

Organizers of teachers groups try to do everything possible to make their members feel safe. They scrupulously guard their mailing lists, schedule meetings in members' homes rather than public places, and do most of their networking by telephone and word-of-mouth. Even so, teachers groups can become targets of antigay threats. Though Massachusetts has some of the most progressive antidiscrimination legislation in the country, including a Governor's Commission on Gay and Lesbian Youth, members of GALE say they have received threats on their answering machine, including this anonymous message: "If I find out where you meet, you're all gonna get fired, you'll never touch my kids."

In places where political tensions are high, teachers groups engage in anguished debates over visibility and safety. During Amendment Two, Michelle Serries recalls, "some teachers were very, very afraid, and wanted the teachers group to absolutely go underground. There were people who actually left the teachers group because they were so afraid." Others, like Michelle and Tracy Phariss, used the group as an organizing base for efforts to oppose the referendum, and later, to help launch the legal challenge that ultimately reached the U.S. Supreme Court.

In Oregon, CUE, the Cascade Union of Educators, has always been relatively low-key, but the more overtly political Educators for Equity was a highly visible participant in the campaign to defeat Ballot Measure Nine in 1992 and Ballot Measure Thirteen in 1994. Ron, the group's past president, thinks their most important contribution was bringing the Oregon Education Association, the statewide branch of the National Education Association, into both campaigns.

In recent years, many teachers groups around the country have begun affiliating with GLSTN, the Gay, Lesbian, and Straight Teachers Network. GLSTN is the first national gay teachers organization; it grew out of a Boston group founded by Concord Academy history teacher Kevin Jennings, who now serves as GLSTN's first executive director. In the introduction to his anthology *One Teacher in Ten*, Kevin writes: "The revolution among gay and lesbian teachers has spread far beyond the places it is 'supposed' to happen."[1] During its short history GLSTN has more than demonstrated the truth of these words, as chapters proliferate around the country.

Torey discovered GLSTN while he was still a Harvard graduate student.

> I was just overwhelmed by being in the presence of gay and lesbian teachers who were out—being able to spend a weekend with each other. There were some who were out, there were some who still weren't out at their schools. But just a weekend to talk with other gay and lesbian teachers about . . . them[selves] as professionals, students at their school, their relationships with their students. It was just a very empowering experience.

By the time Torey moved to Chicago, Kevin Jennings had begun organizing chapters all over the country. Kevin put Torey in contact with two Chicago-area teachers who wanted to start a chapter, and GLSTN/Chicago was born. Though Torey is leaving the Midwest, he plans to become involved with GLSTN/DC when he moves to Montgomery County, Maryland.

Pat Tomaso, another founding member of the Chicago GLSTN chapter, speaks eloquently of the need for a national organization.

---

[1] Kevin Jennings, preface to *One Teacher in Ten: Gay and Lesbian Educators Tell Their Stories* (Boston: Alyson Publications, 1994), p. 12.

I think GLSTN is so important right now. Because more and more of the population are coming to grips with being gay or lesbian a lot earlier in their lives, that's why more and more teachers need to be visible to them, so they have role models, and they get the impression that it's not a bad thing necessarily to be a gay person in this society. . . . By having a national gay teachers organization where teachers can start to feel more comfortable about coming out, students can feel more comfortable about being in the school environment, because there are openly gay and lesbian [teachers] around them to protect them and help them.

Working on the national front has empowered Pat to become more visible in her home community in suburban Chicago. She began volunteering for a local lesbian and gay radio station at the same time she joined GLSTN, and she has also worked for a progressive local candidate, who won election on her second try. Working in this campaign has made Pat feel "for the very first time, as a gay and lesbian person, that I really belong in this community." Pat's political network now includes a group of activist lesbians who meet for coffee once a week. One evening, the women were talking about relationships when a man sitting nearby with his girlfriend jumped into the conversation, and a lively discussion ensued. "In my town," says Pat. "I can't believe it. It feels like I'm just a part of the whole thing, and it's great."

Just across Lake Michigan, Carolyn says that her work with NOW and other national groups helps counteract the isolation she feels in her rural Michigan school. She also attends a lesbian support group in a nearby city, which provides "an outlet where I can be really me and . . . get a lot of support for the hassles I deal with." The group includes other lesbian teachers as well as some lesbian parents who are considering coming out to their children's teachers. "It's been great to discuss those issues," Carolyn says.

Lesbian and gay caucuses of mainstream educational associations have also begun advocating for gay teachers. Paul discovered the lesbian and gay network of the Association for Supervision and Curriculum Development while attending an ASCD conference several years ago. "It was really the first time where I ever met a large number of people all at the same time, with all the same issues to discuss. A really positive experience," he says.

Jan Goodman, who has served as the facilitator of ASCD's lesbian and gay caucus, is also a trainer for the Equity Institute, a diversity leadership organization based in California which runs workshops aimed at ending all forms of oppression. Jan's involvement with Equity has helped her redefine herself as a lesbian teacher and an activist.

There was a time when I was going to make the revolution, and there were only ten people in it. I had one inch of hair, I quit teaching, and I went through this very angry stage—which I think was important, but I'm glad I got to a different place.

All these networks—friends and neighbors, support groups, and teachers organizations—help gay and lesbian teachers feel less alone amid the contradictions of hiding and disclosure. Though they take many forms, support systems remind these teachers of the powerful role that friends and colleagues can play in their lives. Philip Robinson pays eloquent tribute to those who have made his life as a gay teacher more meaningful.

At the age that I'm at, and the things I've gone through, and the many friends that I've lost through AIDS, I think it's the spirit of them that lives through me, to make me be for them who they would want to be. And that's to be out and proud, because in many cases the friends I've lost were out and proud about who they were. Someone still has to speak out and be proud of who we are. . . . Yes, it's going to be a battle, but the battle will be lessened by just standing up and speaking out. . . . So that's the way . . . I carry myself in my daily actions in and around school—and in life.

13

Allies

Jan Goodman and her colleagues at Equity Institute work to empower those without power—gay men and lesbians, women, people with disabilities, and people of color. They also teach people with power how to be allies to others in "target" groups. Becoming allies enables people with privilege to escape the paralyzing bind of guilt. And for those confronting oppression, building coalitions with allies makes it possible to change their lives and their world.

Gay teachers find straight allies in many places—among colleagues and administrators, even among the parents of their students. Straight allies remind gay teachers that they are not alone. Through their actions, they show that they are ready to use their heterosexual privilege to advocate for those who cannot speak out. It is not surprising that gay teachers speak of their straight allies with respect and gratitude.

Many gay teachers say that their most important straight allies are heterosexual colleagues. Deann LeBeau speaks warmly of a woman at her school whom she feels she might even trust with the secret of her identity. "If I were to come out at school and say the 'L' word, I think June would be the person that I would say it to first. June certainly knows who I am."

Some straight allies don't even need to be told. Fran Gardner recalls a colleague who invited her out for a beer one Friday afternoon.

> She said, "I need you to know that I know about your life. I need you to know that I know you're a lesbian, I need you to know that you're safe with me." She had put it all together. . . . Then she said, "It hurts me so much

that you have to live your life the way you do. . . . I just can't believe that your world is like this—and you have my support."

Would-be allies must be ready to listen, and to acknowledge their own homophobia. Soccer coach Dan Woog remembers a dinner conversation with one of his varsity captains, not long after Dan had come out to his school and community.

> At one point he mentioned a kid on the team, and why the other kids didn't like him, and he said that even in elementary school there was an HAF club. "HAF club? What's that?" And he looked stricken. He couldn't speak. He literally couldn't open his mouth. I said, "Chuck? What? What are you talking about?" He said—he choked out the words—"He's a fag club." I said, "I appreciate your discomfort. . . . I'm glad that you realize the power of words."

Principals and other administrators can be vital allies in a gay teacher's life. They are the ones with the power to hire, fire, and defend the teachers who work under their supervision. D. J. Reed has heard plenty of criticism as an out lesbian teacher. But she says she feels safe because of her principal, who told her and the six other gay teachers at her school, "If you get in trouble for being gay they will have to fire me before anybody gets close to you. And I'm not leaving."

Mike Scott describes his principal as an ideal administrator. When he and his partner broke up at the beginning of one school year, she was quick to show her concern.

> She went to my best friend there at the school and told him to keep an eye on me, that something was wrong, she didn't know what. So the next day I took her into her office and told her. She cried and I cried. . . . I love her, she's very highly respected in the district and just a great person.

Terry Minton came out to his principal in response to an article in the student newspaper, which belittled gay men in San Francisco's Castro district and gay people in general. He was determined to say something for the sake of the lesbian and gay students in his school, who remind him of his own painful teenage years. Still, he felt somewhat uncertain about how his principal might respond—a man Terry describes as "the most standard, good ol' boy you could ever find, late fifties, former football coach, small town, redneck background."

I said, "If something like this was written about Black students, it would never be allowed to be published. The only reason you can say it is because no gay kid has got the guts to come in here and say anything, because he'd get killed if he did." I said, "There are 160 gay students in this school." [The school has sixteen hundred students.] And he looked at me like I was going to hand him a list—these are the 160 gay kids.

Despite his apprehension, Terry discovered that his principal wanted to do the right thing.

The principal said, "Oh, I didn't know the kids' situation here. You're right. I was totally insensitive 'cause I didn't see it." . . . He said, "Homosexuality is not something I have had much experience in dealing with before. I don't know their situation. I don't know the faculty situation." And there was a kind of pause, and he said, "I don't know your situation." I said, "I don't have a situation. I'm gay, but that's not a situation for me." I said, "Maybe that's a situation for you that I'm gay."

The principal hardly hesitated before responding.

He said, "The issue would be, are you a different person than the person I love[d] and respect[ed] when you walked into this office? Are you [the] excellent teacher that I've always known you to be?" I was fucking amazed.

Terry was so encouraged by his principal's reaction that he decided to come out to each of the assistant principals, telling them that as a gay man he was concerned about the way lesbian and gay students were treated at school. He continues to be impressed by the fair-mindedness of the principal, who "just by stereotype would be the last person in the world you'd feel safe coming out to."

Administrators can prevent threatening situations from growing into full-scale attacks simply by speaking out quickly and clearly. When a gay teacher was fired at Nancy's school for the Deaf, the administration showed remarkable commitment to the school's other gay and lesbian staff members.

There was one Deaf gay man who had sexually abused the children. . . . So they took him out. . . . They didn't say, "Oh, it's because he's gay." They said, "It's that man. He's a sick man." . . . Some of the parents were afraid and wanted to pull their children out. But the school was very supportive. They said, "It's him. If you're gay, that's fine. If you're a lesbian, that's fine. He was wrong."

Parents, too, can act as straight allies. As Karen's story in Chapter 8 shows, their support can make the difference between a gay teacher's destruction and her survival. Sometimes parent-allies appear in unlikely places, as Allan Arnaboldi discovered during a Massachusetts Gay Pride march.

I'm walking along, and I hear this little voice, "Hi, Allan." And I look up, and one of the kids . . . in my school was on his parent's shoulder. And the mother and father were both marching. And I knew that regardless of why they were there, they were there for a reason that was in support, so after the initial shock, it felt really pretty good.

Claire remembers a supportive parent who became an ally at a time when Claire had just come out and her life as a school counselor seemed very precarious.

The person who did the nicest thing for me was a woman who worked in the kitchen at the school, and whom I had dealt with as a parent. She called me up and said, "I have to talk with you," and drove down to my office and said, "Claire, I just wanted you to know that whatever is going on in your life, it doesn't matter. I still like you as a person." That was wonderful. And nobody else could be so direct.

Students, too, can be allies for their lesbian and gay teachers. D. J. Reed relies on a group of "twenty kids that when things go wrong that involve me, or when I am brought up in a conversation, I know before anyone else knows what's going on." She says:

They're just kids who like me. You know, "Ms. Reed, did you know that so-and-so said you were a dyke?" "Did you know the vice principal is going to observe you today?" . . . It's like a spiderweb with me at the center, and everybody just runs and tells me before they can weave their way back to me.

Jeff says that most of the straight faculty members at his Catholic school are women. He thinks that "creates a different kind of atmosphere." Jeff recalls a conversation he overheard shortly after the publication of the Pope's letter condemning homosexuality.

They started talking about the letter, and how outrageous it was. Discrimination is absolutely wrong, and they thought it was foolish that Catholic teachers couldn't be gay, and all that kind of stuff.

Hearing this conversation was especially reassuring for Jeff, who had only recently come out to himself.

Straight teachers who are members of racial or cultural minorities can be strong allies for their gay colleagues, who can, in turn, become allies against racism. Sue describes an incident that started with two e-mail messages at her Oregon middle school: one contained a snide reference to "the good little fairy," and the other was a racist remark about some Japanese educators who were going to be visiting the school. Sue immediately contacted the only teacher of color in the building, a Japanese woman to whom she had come out earlier that year.

> [I] said to her, "You know there were a couple of comments on e-mail that I wasn't very comfortable with," and explained them, and said, "You know, these don't make me feel very good." . . . And she said, "I'll tell you what. If you fight mine, I'll fight yours."

Nancy, a Deaf White lesbian, has forged a similar alliance with a straight African American teacher at her school.

> I depend on her a lot. She's hearing, and she's Black. So, you know, we understand. We feel kind of the same with our cultures. We support each other a lot.

Heterosexual allies are especially important in the heated atmosphere of antigay political campaigns. Lyn Boudreau still recalls the kindness of her principal, who greeted her the day after Amendment Two was approved by Colorado voters. "She gave me a big shake of the hand, and her eyes filled with tears. She said, "Thank you for what you did.'"

Gay teachers in Oregon were equally grateful to their sympathetic straight colleagues during the Measure Nine and Measure Thirteen campaigns. Martha remembers the straight teachers who wore "No on Nine" buttons in her building. "That felt safe and wonderful, to know that these people . . . didn't approve of discrimination. It felt like a safer place to be."

Barb's straight colleagues showed their support when "Yes on Nine" flyers appeared in their mailboxes.

> At the staff meeting that night somebody stood up and said, "I resent this being in my box, especially anonymously." And so everybody clapped. . . . I felt very supported. . . . I'd been out to my administrator, I knew she absolutely supported me a hundred percent, and . . . there was a strong group of staff members, so I felt very safe. That was really nice.

Chris Nunez relies on many straight allies to help bring her message to students and teachers in San Francisco's public schools. When she first took over the Lesbian and Gay Speakers Bureau, Chris says, it was composed of "two women and seven gay White males." She expanded the number of speakers and recruited lesbians and gay men from San Francisco's Asian, Latino, and Black communities. In the process, Chris developed a host of straight allies in these other communities. She believes that ally building requires careful education, and has organized a series of trainings for members of the speakers bureau.

> My experience throughout my work life in organizations is that you can't mix people without preparing them.... One of our first workshops focused on cross-cultural communication.... One young man ... said, "You know, I want to share something with everybody in this auditorium.... I come from the South, and ... the men in my family used to belong to the Klan." That's the kind of thing that people need to be prepared to understand about, you know, the background that we all come from.... And we all bring that stuff with us.

Chris' insights about coalition building are echoed by Jan Goodman, whose diversity leadership work has given her a profound understanding of the role of allies.

> It's scary to build those alliances. But unless we get together, particularly now, the country's gonna really take a step into the dark ages, and that's frightening to me. 'Cause it's not just gonna be gays.... At every level of school government there are fundamentalists who are putting antigay stuff into the curriculum, and those same people are denying immigrants education and health care.... And unless we get our act together, educators will not have a right to teach anything.

Dan Dromm, who helped organize the first lesbian and gay pride parade in Queens, New York, finds many straight allies in the community where he teaches. "Our parade is held in a community which is overwhelmingly Hispanic, and it's welcomed to the sound of tumultuous applause," he says. Dan adds that the people of color in his school district showed "a tremendous sense of empathy for my cause" during his battle to retain the multicultural literature curriculum, including books depicting gay and lesbian families, in his district.

Straight allies can be colleagues and neighbors, but they can also be strangers who speak out as a matter of principle. Carolyn Wood still remembers a straight ally she met at a conference several years ago.

There was a meeting of gay and lesbian [educators] and somebody there spoke and said that . . . being straight gives you a different kind of power in the school system. . . . That it was the responsibility of straight teachers. . . . That was just very inspiring to me. I came back and talked to several friends, and said, "This really makes sense."

Heterosexual teachers, parents, and administrators who want to improve the lives of gay and lesbian teachers would do well to heed Carolyn's words. Heterosexuality does indeed carry "a different kind of power" in a heterosexist world. By exercising that power—speaking out against homophobia, letting lesbian and gay colleagues know they are valued, challenging stereotypes wherever they appear—straight allies can hasten the day when their gay and lesbian colleagues will be free to speak out for themselves.

PART FIVE

From Survival to Empowerment

"When we started, I wasn't even going to Gay Pride, I was so scared of the whole thing. And then I marched in the parade with a hat on, and sunglasses. And now it's just walking down the street with the educators, without a care in the world, and some old students who are gay saying 'Hi, Barb, we love you!'"

Barb, *middle school teacher, Oregon*

14

Speaking Out

COMING OUT AS A LESBIAN OR GAY MAN IS A RITE OF PAS-
sage, a moment of truth, a step toward integration. It is also a process. Nam-
ing oneself as lesbian, gay, or bisexual is only the beginning, followed by a
continuing series of disclosures to family, friends, coworkers, and acquaintances. And coming out does not end after a gay person has shared his or her
gay identity with others; it continues with every new colleague or friend,
neighborhood or work environment. Since our society takes heterosexuality
for granted, gay people must constantly come out if they are to be seen as who
really are. Such disclosure is sometimes called "flaunting" by heterosexuals;
yet if homosexuality were the norm, what straight person would not want to
be sure everyone knew that he or she was heterosexual?

Gay teachers who cannot say "I am gay," or "I am lesbian," or "I am
bisexual," still find ways to say, "I am here." They introduce curriculum materials that promote diversity. They invite guest speakers to their classrooms
and staff workshops, and establish classroom rules that prohibit homophobic
name-calling. While these initiatives do not entirely liberate teachers from the
closet, they help create a safe environment for gay students and teachers.

Challenging stereotypes is one important way that gay teachers tell the
truth about themselves, even when they cannot explicitly come out. Karen
insists on educating her Maine junior high school students about the isolation of gay adolescents ("I do my little talk about gay teens at least three times
a year"), and about the high suicide rate among lesbian and gay youth.

> We have had any number of conversations about the fact that they know
> people, whether they know it or not, [who] are gay and lesbian. Ten percent

of every group is going to be gay or lesbian. That they have relatives who are gay or lesbian that they might not know are. That they at some point are going to be at school with kids who are gay and lesbian—and I look around the room and say, "if you aren't already."

Teachers at the elementary level find it appropriate to challenge stereotypes about gender roles that lead to homophobic attitudes later on. Doralynn says her kindergartners and first graders arrive with the assumption that "boys wear blue and play with trucks, and girls must have dresses and [wear] pink." At this age, she says, "they just love learning," and she finds it easy to present more open ideas, "to instill these little things in their minds."

Jan Goodman recalls that even the preschoolers in the Cambridge, Massachusetts, alternative school where she began her teaching career came with established ideas about gender roles. One day, they were acting out *Sleeping Beauty*, and wanted her to play the prince.

I said, "Well, no, I can't really be the prince, I'm female, but I'd be the princess." And they said, "Oh, no, ooh, yuck. The princess can't wake up Sleeping Beauty. It has to be a prince." I said, "Well, I can't help you then." And they went around and . . . none of the boys would do it, and then finally they came back again and they said, "Okay, you could be the princess." So I woke up Sleeping Beauty, and one of them apparently went home and told her mother, "You know, it doesn't always have to be a prince."

Jan's experience shows how a teacher can help change stereotypes in young minds, but it also provides a reminder that students are likely to repeat their teachers' words to parents who may or may not be sympathetic. Lourdes says she knows her fifth graders talk to their parents about what goes on in her classroom.

Parents always come to open house and they say, "They talk about you at dinner all the time, my teacher said this and my teacher said that." And you just wait for something to be taken out of context. That's the kind of thing that I'm really afraid of.

Even Lyn Boudreau, who is completely out to her students and staff, sometimes worries about how others interpret her classroom comments.

I've heard rumbling of some kids who've labeled me maybe partial to queers because I would say something about it. That was kind of hard at times, 'cause I knew some teachers didn't say anything because they were afraid of being labeled.

Lyn points out that gay teachers can feel very isolated when they are the only adults who interrupt homophobic name-calling. "I'd hear games called 'Smear the Queer,'" she says. "A lot of teachers wouldn't say anything, but I knew that I needed to say something."

One of the most effective ways to create a safe classroom environment is to establish rules early in the year and enforce them consistently. Rules prohibiting homophobic language and behavior are a way for lesbian and gay teachers to demand respect for themselves and their gay students without drawing attention to themselves. Cary gives his elementary school students "four expectations: to listen, communicate, solve problems, and respect self and others." Jean Bourg establishes a similar code for her high school computer students: "Classroom rule: no put-down of any minority groups, [no using] the word 'nigger' and the word 'dyke' and—I do enforce that— 'faggot.'"

Alice is lucky to teach in a school with a buildingwide policy against discrimination. "We have a classroom covenant that we use as our school rules. . . . We treat each other with respect, we won't call each other names."

Teachers with strong classroom rules against name-calling find that even though their students may complain, they abide by these rules, and even internalize them. Pam says:

> I feel real good about the fact that other people come back to me who had kids actually say, "You wouldn't get away with that in Miss Bradbury's class." Kids feel real safe and clear about what the expectations are.

Karen's eighth graders know she does not tolerate homophobic slurs. "At lunchtime . . . I keep tabs on all the conversations, and if I hear, 'fag' or something, it's like—'Robert?' Then I hear, 'Sorry, Miss Stone!' . . . I hear them saying, 'S-s-s-h!' 'Oh, I forgot.'"

Carolyn prohibits certain homophobic expressions in her classroom, like, "That's so gay."

> A lot of kids now are so used to it that when they say that, they immediately look up and say, "I'm sorry, Miss Whitney." Not because they understand that I'm gay, but because they know they're going to get a detention.

Though a well-enforced classroom code can help create a safe and respectful environment, gay-baiting has become so common in schools that most teachers cannot avoid directly confronting students about offensive remarks. As Anne says, "It's sort of replaced giving people the finger—the verbal finger."

Karen Cosper began confronting homophobic slurs during the Measure Nine campaign in Oregon.

If kids were calling another kid a queer on the playground, I would talk to the entire classroom about it, say that some of my very best friends in the whole world are gay or lesbian, and that when you use that in a hurtful way, that it hurts people and it hurts me.

Some teachers adopt an impersonal strategy. Jessie says that as a permanent substitute teacher, she was exposed to "a side of kids that nobody else sees—the lowest level." Her upper-middle-class students felt they "had to keep the racial comments [at a] very low level," but were overtly homophobic.

If two girls were walking together, other girls would bump into them and scream "Dykes" at them. I would hear kids say, "I wish all gay people were dead, they should all be killed."

Jessie usually stepped in, even though she was not the regular teacher.

I constantly confronted the students and said, "I will not accept any kind of jokes against race, religion, and sexual orientation." And they would say, "Why? Are you gay?" And I would say, "Why? Because I don't believe in hate."

Teachers who want their students to understand the power of name-calling remind them that lesbian and gay people may be among their peers. Julie tells her students:

You may think you're kidding but that's not the perception other people have. You may have hurt somebody else's feelings just 'cause you're kidding with your buddy over here.

Dianne informs students who call each other "queer" that they need to use a more appropriate word. "Sometimes I'll say to a person, 'What if that person is gay? How do you think it makes them feel?'"

Alice follows up her school's antislur policy with her own direct interventions. "I try to work on discrimination with everybody," she says. "I mean, don't do it. It's just not right. How would you feel?" Alice's students have responded to her direct appeals to fairness, even if they have not completely abandoned the stereotypes.

One kid has actually said, "I'll never be a fag and I don't understand it, but I won't beat on anybody anymore because I know it's wrong. . . . And that's all 'cause of you." And I said, "No, it's 'cause of you. I just provided a little entryway into the world, and [to] looking at yourself."

Some educators, like Anne, challenge homophobic remarks with a literal approach that puts the perpetrator on the spot.

I'll say, "What do you mean? The person is a homosexual?" "No, no, no. That's not what I mean." "Well, what do you mean? All right. Well, let's get what you really mean, and not just use that term."

Karen uses the literal approach on the school playground, where she frequently sees fifth- and sixth-grade girls holding hands on the swings, and hears their classmates calling them "lezzies."

I ask them what is wrong with what they are doing. "Well, they look like two lezzies." "Is that so bad?" I ask. "It looks to me like they are good friends. Do they really look like they are sexual? Is this your concern?" "No, they don't." "Well," I say, "let's not use that word, let's not even talk about people this way, please." I've told them they can talk about lesbians and gay men, but they are to call them lesbians and gay men.

Judi uses the same strategy with her second and third graders.

Recently . . . a boy called somebody else gay, and I said, "Do you know what the word means?" He said, "Yes, it's when a man loves another man or a woman loves another woman." I said, "That's wonderful. You know that and you can express that so positively." But then when we continued to go on about name-calling, we had to explore some other issues.

Hope says that humor can often defuse the tension around homophobic name-calling.

I heard a kid saying the other day that he didn't want to go near this boy because the boy was homo. I said, "Do you think you can catch stuff like that?" And he's like, "I don't know. I don't want to take the chance." I'm like, "Oh, you know, you have to be careful." Even adults I've done that to. Because there are a lot of stupid adults too.

In recent years, AIDS jokes and AIDS-phobia have created a new variety of name-calling. Alan Kelly-Hamm addressed one such remark with a personal response.

A fairly close friend of ours . . . died the day before school started. The day after I came back from the memorial service, one of the second graders started making AIDS jokes, "You've got AIDS," which was common. I took him aside and I said I had a friend who just died of AIDS, and I came back from his memorial service and I really don't like that joke. "You need to think about the fact that there may be people here who have family or friends with AIDS, and it's not a funny joke. Do you know what AIDS is?" "No." He knew, but he wasn't going to say it. I said, "It's a disease that people get, and it's not just a gay thing."

Peggy chose a literature unit to address the subject of AIDS in her high school English classroom.

The minister of my church read a book called *The Screaming Room*. . . . It's a mother's journal of [her son's] decline and death from AIDS. I read the book and I couldn't think of anything else for days. . . . And of course, you can't deal with AIDS without getting into all the issues surrounding homophobia. You have people making incredibly ignorant comments, and you have to deal with them. So that was a door.

Peggy taught *The Screaming Room* soon after she had become aware of her own sexual orientation. At that time, she says, she felt more self-conscious than she would have earlier in her career. "But every time I started to get a little nervous about it, I said to myself, 'How would I have handled this if it had been five years ago? I wouldn't have done it any differently.'"

Peggy's courage to tackle the subject of AIDS—and homophobia—in her classroom came from what she calls "the urgent mission to be in the thick of it." The same mission moves lesbian and gay teachers to confront homophobia not only in their classrooms, but in the teachers lounge, the cafeteria, and the hallways of their schools. "I correct kids whether I have them or not," says Gary. "I always correct kids. I correct kids at the grocery store."

Coming out in school, as in every other part of a gay person's life, is as much a state of mind as it is a statement. The process begins when gay teachers learn to value themselves as gay people and educators. And it continues as they come to believe that the personal costs of hiding are greater than the risks of self-disclosure. Jean Bourg says:

As a matter of my self-protection, it's simply easier to be semi-out than it is to be closeted. I am prepared to make a stand if it comes to that, and I think when you are prepared to make a stand, you are less likely to have to make one. . . . I realize at some point that I will tell them explicitly and they are going to have to put that together somehow with the person that they know.

Pam talks about the importance of the person-to-person connection. "It's a lot easier to hate somebody that's not a human being than to look someone straight in the eyes and say the same thing." For Pam, moving out of the closet is both an obligation and a step toward self-empowerment.

> I feel that if you don't go to places that are difficult you allow that situation to become more and more difficult. . . . We do a disservice to ourselves to remain closeted. And the only way to change it is to be there.

During the Amendment Two campaign, Tracy Phariss told his Denver seventh graders that if the amendment passed, he could lose his job.

> We did a sample poll, just like a regular election. My team voted Amendment Two down. That's one hundred and fifty kids. The other team, which I was not on, voted for it. . . . The kids on my team couldn't believe it passed. . . . On the other team, name-calling was greater after Amendment Two.

Remembering the debates among Colorado's gay teachers during those months, Tracy sees the campaign as a turning point in his own awareness.

> A lot of teachers said, "Well, we shouldn't be getting involved because this is a political activity." . . . They would still volunteer their time, but it would be not as a teacher, just as a gay man. They have difficulty in correlating the two. You can't just be a teacher. You have to be a teacher and a gay man. You can't just be a gay man. You're also a teacher by heart.

Gwen thinks about these questions as she prepares to return to teaching after a leave of absence.

> If they ask me if I'm gay, I probably won't lie. . . . I really believe in honesty, and I believe if you put things out there in the right attitude and the right way, and if you're not out there to just be self-centered or to be self-seeking or to put anybody down—that what goes around comes around. . . . Either you become really stifled and closeted or you start to really live your politics.

Coming out in school, Gwen thinks, is not all that different from coming out in other parts of life. "Either everything gets easier for you, or [it gets] harder temporarily, and then it gets easier again."

Tracy, Pam, Jean, and Gwen consider coming out in school a moral imperative and a strategic necessity. Their words apply to all teachers who have come out to colleagues and administrators, challenged homophobic behavior, and incorporated lesbian and gay perspectives into their classroom curricula. But they are just as relevant to teachers like Michael, who is only beginning the process. "I definitely want to be more out," he says. "It's my last closet. And I don't think I'm gonna feel one hundred percent okay until I don't have closets in my life."

15

Moving Out

IN A POIGNANT LYRIC, SINGER/SONGWRITER FRED SMALL describes a lesbian teacher named Annie who spends her days keeping her distance from her students, "avoiding the personal pronoun," and "never letting out too much of her life." She endures the pitying whispers of her colleagues, who wonder, "What are we gonna do about Annie?" and keep trying to help her find the right man. In the last verse, Annie sits by the fire with her lover, "and imagines the day/ When she'll look in their faces" and tell everybody that "Annie's doing just fine."

Annie's fantasy arises from her desire to be seen whole, and to have her primary relationship freely acknowledged. It is a fantasy shared by virtually all gay teachers, no matter how closeted they may be at school. For most, it remains an ideal waiting in the distant future, or a dream they hope will come true for the next generation of teachers.

But for a few lesbian and gay educators, surviving and thriving as an openly gay teacher is more than a dream. They have discovered the paradox at the heart of the gay liberation movement: self-revelation is the riskiest act imaginable for someone who is gay, lesbian, or bisexual, yet at the same time, it holds the greatest potential for true liberation.

Coming out in school is not always a single, dramatic event. Sometimes, it is a gradual process during which teachers test the waters, and reassure themselves that the support is there.

Michelle began coming out at her school for the Deaf by self-disclosing to a few trusted colleagues. During her first year, she met most of the lesbian and gay faculty, and came out to a few straight allies. In the fall of her second year, a group of women teachers invited her on a camping trip to Yosemite.

Deciding to go on that trip was kind of deciding to be out to that group of people, because I would want to bring Denise [her partner]. . . . I wanted to make sure no one would flip out about it because we were all staying in one little trailer. So I did let people know beforehand. I said, "My girlfriend's going to come with us."

Everyone on the trip was friendly and accepted Michelle and Denise as a couple. After that, Michelle says, "it felt a lot freer. I just slowly started coming out to people. And just slowly started censoring myself less and less." Eventually, she reached the point where she didn't care who else found out—"and that was a big relief." She distinguishes between being explicitly out to a few colleagues, and being implicitly (or explicitly) out to an entire community.

It's different to choose your people you want to be out to, but once you've decided you don't care who else knows, then you can talk about things at lunch without worrying who's looking over and watching. . . . When you go into a restaurant, you don't worry if you run into someone, if people overhear things, or if you wear a piece of jewelry that someone recognizes as gay jewelry.

Later that fall, a question from one of her ninth graders precipitated the final stage in Michelle's coming out.

I was teaching a unit on censorship and banned books, preceding teaching *Catcher in the Rye*, and I was getting the kids all infuriated that books could be banned, and talking about the right to truth, the right to knowledge, and the right for teenagers to be treated the same way as adults and be given the honest truth.

During a break after the first part of the class, one girl lingered near the front desk.

She said, "Can I ask you a personal question?" And I'm thinking, "Oh-oh." As gay teachers always think when they hear that. She said, "Two questions. First of all, are you married?" And I said, "No." And then she said, "Are you a lesbian?" She was giggling. She said, "There have been some rumors. We're wondering." And I couldn't think of any response other than the truth, especially after having just done this whole thing on censorship. So I said very calmly, "Yes," and I think she was kind of surprised at my honesty. . . . She said, "Oh, okay, thanks." And she ran out of the room and ran up to a friend of hers from another class who was waiting down the hall for her response.

The next day, Michelle wondered if what would happen in her class-room. "Knowing kids, it takes only three minutes for the whole school to know something," she observes, "especially in the Deaf community." But everything proceeded just as it always had.

The kids who were obnoxious were still obnoxious, the kids who were good were still good. Nothing happened. And I waited for, like days and weeks, and weeks, and nothing happened.

Michelle thinks that the tone of her coming out had a lot to do with the students' response.

I felt like it was really important to be honest and to show that it was not a big deal. It was just part of who I was, and I wasn't ashamed of it. . . . I felt really strongly that there was nothing wrong with what I had done. I had been asked a question and I had answered honestly.

Later that year, the school psychologist told Michelle about a boy who had come for counseling not long after Michelle had come out to her students. Though the counselor could not divulge the boy's identity, Michelle has a good idea who he might be.

My guess was, it was a kid I had referred to counseling. He had written some suicidal poetry, and I had pretty strong suspicions that he was gay and maybe having a hard time with it. . . . I had specifically referred him to a counselor that I knew was supportive. . . . He said to her, "I'm gay, but it's okay, because there's a high school teacher who is too."

Hearing this story, Michelle knew she had done the right thing. "I felt like if my coming out had made a difference like that to one kid, it was worth it if I got fired." But she did not get fired. Her relationships with administrators and colleagues remained unchanged, except that working with an openly lesbian colleague forced some of them to examine their own attitudes.

The hardest things came from the staff that I was closer to, because I pushed their limits and kind of forced them to deal with it more. I had some con-versations with a couple of straight colleagues trying to get them to under-stand what it was like to be a lesbian in that kind of environment, and how even though they might not go around talking about being heterosexual, in their everyday expressions it was there, by wearing a wedding ring or hav-ing a picture up or even saying, "My husband had the flu yesterday." There were ways in which I was still closeted if I wasn't talking about that.

Being explicitly out to faculty and students has reduced Michelle's anxiety, but it has not ended the coming-out process.

These people who act like they really like me, I wonder if they know, and it makes me wish they knew. I hope they're acting this way already knowing. I also hope people know so that people realize how many lesbians there are, and that we look like every different walk of life. . . . The only time it's uncomfortable is when I walk into a restaurant with my girlfriend, and I see a whole clan of people from school and I wonder if this is sort of like I'm coming out to them, or it's no big deal because they already knew.

Teaching as an out lesbian has been gratifying for Michelle, and, she believes, for all of her straight and gay students.

I think there's a way in which lesbians experience a lot of oppression, and I think that teenagers experience a lot of oppression, and I think in a way it lets me relate to the kids on a certain level. . . . And I also feel like on the other side of being scared and being closeted, when you come out and you feel like you've done something really brave, it can feel really exciting. And I like the idea that all thirty of the students I taught this year now have met a lesbian and now have spent a year in a classroom every single day making jokes and having arguments and learning things, and just being normal with a lesbian. I really like the idea.

Alejandra Dubove's coming-out story resembles Michelle's in several ways. Both young women began by coming out to a few colleagues; both came out to students during their second year of teaching; and both experienced positive responses from staff and students. Alejandra's coming out was prompted by indignation: she was angry at her colleagues' failure to support Chris Huff, the lesbian teacher who had been denied permission to live with her partner, and whose lawsuit had been the subject of Alejandra's first conversation with the headmaster. Early in her first year, Alejandra learned more about Chris Huff.

Supposedly she had a lot of friends at the school, and people really supported her, and at our staff meeting one of the teachers would give updates on what was going on with the lawsuit, and nobody ever said anything. I felt, this is weird. I mean, if people are so into civil rights and support her, and even had a personal friendship with her—and nobody says anything? So I started voicing my opinion about it more, and lost a couple of, well, whatever—I guess, friends.

After Chris Huff lost her case, Alejandra began coming out to more staff members. At this point, she considers that she was "implicitly out."

I had my bumper stickers on my car. My pink triangles on my jacket. Some literature up. Kids asked me directly, some kids asked me, "Are you a lesbian?" and I said, "Yeah." But I would never like announce it.

In November of her second year, Alejandra attended a GLSTN retreat where each teacher was asked to set a goal.

I said, "My goal is to come out to my classes," but I didn't know how I was going to do that. And then in December I changed my curriculum. "It's World AIDS Day, we have to think about this."

Alejandra began by showing the film *And the Band Played On,* which traces the origin of the AIDS crisis in the 1980s. Afterward, students discussed various issues raised in the film, and the subject turned to gays in the military.

I said, "Take, for example, me, I can never be in the military." And they were like, "Why?" I said, "Well, because I'm a lesbian." And suddenly the kids were like, "Oh. Well, my uncle's gay." Another kid said, "Oh, you know, k.d. lang's a lesbian." Another kid said, "Oh, one of my friends is gay. He's really a nice guy." . . . They started asking all sorts of questions. "What's it like being gay?" "Did anybody ever discriminate against you?" "Is that your girlfriend in that picture in your office?" Things like that.

From then on, Alejandra says, "We were so close. It's probably the best thing I ever did with my kids." She continued to come out to her other classes.

Every time I did it I'd be sweating, I'd be so scared, like, oh, shit, they're going to freak out, think I'm a pervert, I'll get phone calls from parents. And none of that happened. Not once.

Coming out of the closet opened other doors, some metaphoric and some real.

Suddenly everything that I kept in my office went out in the hall. All the gay posters, affirmations, and gay history things. It was like I opened my door and I said, "Look, I've got *Bay Windows* [a Boston gay and lesbian newspaper] at the school, I don't need to hide it anymore. Here's *Bay Windows,* here's *OUT* magazine, let's get some supports for the kids." . . . I had kids come to me to tell me all sorts of problems, coming-out anxieties, or things they're dealing with at home or with their friends and families. . . . I had thirty-five kids request me to be their advisor for next year and I could only take five.

Despite all the positive responses, Alejandra was nervous about coming out to her Latino students.

> There aren't that many Latino kids at our school. So it's already special to have a teacher who's Spanish. They come to me, we can relate to one another. . . . I can talk to them in Spanish and we have our little jokes. I thought if I came out to them, suddenly that would be gone, because I wasn't their Spanish teacher or their friend or somebody they could talk to, but the whole negative energy behind being gay or lesbian, which is a really negative energy in the Latino community. . . . And it didn't happen.

At the end of the year, Alejandra read her students' evaluations of her courses. The two curriculum units that received the most praise were *The Times of Harvey Milk,* the documentary film about the life and death of San Francisco's first gay Supervisor; and *Becoming Visible,* a lesbian and gay history reader by GLSTN founder Kevin Jennings.

Alejandra's visibility as a gay teacher has brought new responsibilities as well as new freedoms. As the only out gay teacher at the school (and one of only two minority teachers), she has been appointed the school's diversity director for next year.

> I have the whole year planned out. We're having Gay History Month. And we're also going to recognize National Coming Out Day. I realize I'm going to have to be the role model for that. So I'm gonna have to go to assembly and talk about coming out. . . . It's going to be really terrifying. But it has to be done, because I'm still hearing kids say, "faggot," or "that's gay," or "dyke."

And as long as there are negative images in her school, Alejandra says, she will be coming out to students at Chapel Hill–Chauncey Hall. She encourages other gay teachers to do the same.

> That creates a bond that is very powerful, and I think in the more individualized level it's more effective in breaking down stereotypes or fears or misconceptions. I can pass out literature and you can read it, but then when it's somebody you know and you talk to them, it makes all the difference.

There were no lawsuits pending when Doyle Forister came out at Skyview High School in Billings, Montana, but the events were almost as sudden and certainly as dramatic. In 1993, Doyle was teaching an evening course on sexual diversity at a local college, and had led a workshop on gay youth. A local TV reporter asked him if he would be willing to be interviewed, Doyle consented, and they did a "real rich background talk" about the issues raised in his course. The reporter assured Doyle that his sexual orientation would not be identified, and during the interview, he says, "we did not discuss my sexuality at all."

That night, the piece appeared on TV as "an interview with a local educator who is gay." The news anchor had rewritten the reporter's introduction. "So," Doyle says, "I got outed in the eastern half of the state to northern Wyoming. . . . It [felt like] the worst thing that had happened to me up until that point, [but] it's been the best thing that has happened to me."

As soon as the program appeared, a local right-wing religious group phoned the school and demanded Doyle's resignation.

> Fortunately, my credentials had been established for two decades. People came up and let me know that, "Hey, what a person does in their own time, we don't think they need to be labeled, and so, you know, we won't mention it." I said, "Why not?" I bring it up, I joke about it.

The next morning, Doyle met with his principal and explained what had happened. Because he had been out to the principal for over two years, the issue was not his sexual orientation, but the bad judgment of the news anchor in rewriting the reporter's story. Once the principal understood the truth, he was able to respond to the many telephone calls that came in that day. In addition, Doyle says, the reporter wrote a "glowing" letter of apology to him in care of the superintendent and the school board. "She said that she only hoped the other educators in the district were as dedicated to the good of kids as I was."

Doyle says that there were no negative repercussions in his school. "They say if everybody would come out, it would just make the difference. Well, just one person coming out makes a big difference."

Doyle has continued to speak out about homophobia, especially about the needs of lesbian and gay youth. He has presented workshops at the state teachers conference, taught courses on sexual diversity in his district, and hosted a regional P-FLAG meeting that attracted people from all over Montana and northern Wyoming. In 1993, Doyle's activism as an openly gay teacher in Billings involved him in a remarkable chapter in American civil rights history.

A year earlier, hate literature had begun appearing in Billings, signed by people claiming to be members of the Ku Klux Klan. Shortly before Rosh Hashanah, the Jewish New Year, nineteen headstones in the Jewish cemetery were pushed over, and the words "Nuke Israel" appeared on a stop sign near the synagogue that serves the town's one hundred Jewish residents. At about the same time, worshippers at the African Methodist Episcopal Wayman

Chapel were harassed by three White men who entered the church and stood, arms crossed, during services; a Native American resident had her home painted with a swastika; and a beer bottle was thrown through the glass door of the home of Uri Barnea, the music director of the Billings Symphony and a child of Holocaust survivors. Lesbians and gays were among those harassed; in March 1994, a Billings artist returned home from an out-of-town trip to find a swastika and the word "fag" spray painted on his property.

The culminating attack came in early December, when someone threw a brick at the home of a Jewish couple, Brian and Tammie Schnitzer. The Schnitzers had placed a menorah in their window, in celebration of the upcoming Hanukkah holiday; the brick left a hail of shattered glass on the bed of the Schnitzers' young son Isaac, who was not in his room at the time.

What followed has become almost a legend for human rights activists around the country. Within a few weeks, paper menorahs appeared in thousands of windows in Billings. The inspiration came from Margaret MacDonald, a Protestant who remembered the story of how the Danish king and his countrymen donned yellow stars to show their solidarity with Denmark's Jews during the Nazi occupation. A few days later, the Universal Athletic Service, a local sports equipment store, posted a new message on the large sign in its parking lot: NOT IN OUR TOWN! NO HATE. NO VIOLENCE. PEACE ON EARTH. And on December 10, the Billings Human Rights Coalition, an organization that had been founded in 1992, held a candlelight vigil outside the synagogue, where members of the community denounced the violence that had targeted the minority citizens of Billings.

Doyle Forister attended that candlelight vigil, and has been actively involved in Billings' fight against hate crimes. As an openly gay teacher, he is especially aware of the vulnerability of gays and lesbians. When hate literature began appearing on cars and in mailboxes, Doyle's friends were among those listed by name.

> Some had their names listed on these fliers . . . put out by branches of the Klan, the Klan of America . . . saying the Bible talks about helping these people out of their tortured souls with castration and a knife across the throat. These things are very violent and they were listing names of friends of mine in town.

Because of the efforts of Doyle and other gay activists, the Billings human rights network realized that lesbians and gays were as much at risk as other minorities in their town. "The Jewish community spoke up and said . . . we should address the needs of gays and lesbians too," Doyle says. "It brought together factions within the community that would not naturally have been there."

When the crew of CBS Sunday Morning came to Billings to film a segment on the story, the Schnitzers "made a point of emphasizing to them and to the rest of the community" that lesbians and gay men were among the victims of hate crimes in Billings, and that the BHRC opposed homophobia along with racism and anti-Semitism. Unfortunately, this part of the interview was edited out of the final show, an omission that Doyle feels speaks volumes about the invisibility of homophobic violence in the American media.

By early 1994, hate crimes had ebbed in Billings. The perpetrators have never been found. Though the atmosphere is still tense, Doyle sees what happened there as a victory for the BHRC, and for the citizens who stood in solidarity with their Jewish, African American, Native American, and lesbian and gay neighbors. Like many others, he attributes the victory to the active support of community leaders who declared publicly that violence against some members of a community hurts all. What happened in Billings is an object lesson in the power of allies; but the lesbian and gay community probably would have been far less visible if not for the presence of Doyle Forister. And Doyle says that he would never have been as successful as a visible gay teacher and human rights activist without his allies, the principal and staff of Skyview High School.

> The only reason I have any sense of mental health and well-being is because of my principal . . . who is from a very conservative religious background. But part of his Christian background is that you take care of your own life and you don't judge others. . . . It's a phenomenal blessing.

Coming out on TV took Doyle Forister by surprise; for poet Alan Miller, teaching in the Bay Area of California, it was no surprise to find himself featured on a PBS documentary late in 1989. For several years, Alan had been part of a group of gay African American men who included the late film producer Marlon Riggs, then a professor at the University of California at Berkeley. Tongues Untied, Riggs' most controversial film, featured the men in the group talking about race and racism, sexuality, and HIV. (The film later became the focal point of the battle by Jesse Helms and others to withdraw government funding from the National Endowment for the Arts; many PBS stations refused to air it because of its frank discussion of sexuality.)

When Tongues Untied appeared on Bay Area public television, Alan was in his first year of teaching at Richmond High School. At that point, he had not come out explicitly to the staff or the students.

There were lots of people who were there to talk with me about the film, and when I walked into the area leading to the classrooms . . . there was all this whispering. . . . A couple of people came up to ask me if I was in a film. . . . Then my department chair came in. . . . She said, "Were you on television last night?"

Students in Alan's morning classes did not mention the film, but by later in the day word had gotten around. A few students had seen the program; others had heard about it and wanted to ask questions.

They said they wanted to see it as a class. And months later, I brought it. I showed it to them. It was fine. Some people were really disgusted by or had visceral responses to some parts, and I was disgusted at their disgust. . . . I had them write things rather than just say them. And I found out some remarkable things. One of the students—his mom was a lesbian, other students had gay siblings. I found out later that one of the students was herself a lesbian. She didn't write that down then, but she said that it was very important to her, that she wanted to be a teacher and that it was very important to be out as a teacher.

The following year, Alan brought Marlon Riggs to school as a guest speaker. "He came to all five classes over a period of two days, and all the classes except one were good."

By the time Alan left Richmond, he felt confident enough to be out in his job interviews.

One of the committees was a group of three White men, and they did all their questions and they asked me if I had any questions. I said, "Yes. I'm an openly gay teacher and I deal with these things in the classroom." And I said, "Who else on your faculty deals with these issues?"

The administration at this school offered Alan a job; so did another school where he came out during his job interview. So did Berkeley High School, where he has been teaching English for the past four years. There, he says, he has been "both comfortable and uncomfortable."

I don't come out in a sexual way. When I come out to students in my classes, I bring out my books. I may bring out pictures of me, awards. . . . This is who I am and this is some of the work that I do. . . . I've been here four years, so it's not a big surprise.

Nevertheless, Alan's life as an openly gay teacher has not been without incident. A year ago, someone broke into his classroom and painted homophobic slogans across the walls. Teachers have made comments behind his back, Alan says, and students have made homophobic remarks in the hallways. Administrators have varied in their responses to these incidents. "Some counselors and vice principals think that people should be disciplined for saying, 'Fuck you, faggot.' Others don't think that at all."

Despite the harassment, Alan continues to raise the consciousness of his students and faculty by teaching works with gay characters and themes, bringing lesbian and gay guest speakers to class, and speaking out against the harassment of lesbian and gay students. One measure of his success is the number of openly gay teachers at Berkeley High. Today, he says, there are seven or eight; when Alan arrived four years ago, there were none. Making the school safer for all gay teachers and students is part of what Alan calls "stretching the boundaries."

John Anderson and Dan Woog are Connecticut educators who both came out in local newspaper columns. Both have found school and community support for their decisions to teach as openly gay men. They have an additional connection: John appears in Dan's book, *School's Out: The Impact of Gay and Lesbian Issues on America's Schools.*

John Anderson teaches Latin at two Stratford, Connecticut, high schools. He lives in the town of Woodbridge, twenty miles away, with his partner, Garrett Stack, an elementary school principal. In 1992, John was offered the opportunity to take over a *New Haven Register* column on lesbian and gay issues. He accepted the offer, partly, he says, out of "an intense love of writing," but mostly out of "a growing dissatisfaction with hiding and being only partly alive at work. . . . It was just time for me." A month earlier, John had fought a battle with his principal, who thought that John's self-defined official goal for the year, "to examine the needs of gay and lesbian kids," was "totally inappropriate." Writing for the *Register* would be a way of bringing these needs out into the open, not only to the two high schools but to the community as well.

When he submitted his first column, John thought he'd have a few months to prepare himself and his colleagues for its publication, but the piece appeared almost immediately. "I was at lunch and a teacher handed me the paper and said she had been given it by another colleague and he had been given it by an administrator from the central office across town." Seeing himself out in print hit John "like a sock in the stomach, and I just needed a little time off by myself to digest this new information."

Colleagues' reactions were generally positive.

There were a lot of strange looks, some hostile looks, but a lot of very supportive talk. People coming up and making a point of patting me on the back and saying, "Hey, I read your column. . . . I really like what you're doing."

John's decision to come out empowered him and his colleagues "to talk about the issue for the first time." Even his principal acknowledged that something needed to be done to confront homophobia at the school. At the end of the school year, John received a human relations award from his teachers union at a banquet attended by more than three hundred teachers, along with the administration and the board of education.

Since coming out, John has encouraged the student newspapers at both schools to publish articles on gay and lesbian issues. He and his partner bought a half-page ad affirming lesbian and gay youth in each of the yearbooks. He has helped found EdFlag, Connecticut Educators and Friends of Lesbians and Gays. And John's column has continued to appear, keeping the issue of lesbian and gay identity alive in the wider world.

Shortly after John's columns began appearing in the *Register*, the editor of the student newspaper in Woodbridge asked him to write an article.

The very day that it came out, I got a death threat from, I would say, a junior- or senior-age male high school student from here in town. . . . I got another one a few days later. . . . And also that same day that the article came out in the school paper in Woodbridge, a member of the school board in Woodbridge showed up at Stratford High asking "if this is where the gay teacher worked."

Why did people in the two towns react so differently? John thinks it is because people in the Stratford schools knew and liked him, while in Woodbridge he was an unknown quantity.

What I relied on heavily in the school system is that they knew me for six years or more, and I had a good reputation, I get along well with people. If you've got that to bank on, it really puts the burden on them to do something about how they feel about gays. . . . Those kids at the high school here [in Woodbridge] don't know me. I may live in town, but that doesn't mean anything. I'm some stranger who's intruded into their school with an article, and they lashed out. Whereas the kids that I work with, they've seen me or worked with me day after day, or their friends had me in class.

Receiving threatening phone calls has taken its toll on John's physical and emotional health.

I've been to the doctor a few times to get medication for an incipient ulcer, I've lost some sleep over it, I've been afraid to sit at the dining room table, where I always sit with my back to the window facing the street. I've had to have lights on outside for a while. . . . It really unnerves you. The cops said, "Take it seriously. Don't assume it's a crank. Just assume it's for real."

Nevertheless, John says that given the choice, he would do it again, "in a minute. Because I've seen the results, which are a heightened awareness. . . . The more of us that do this, the more . . . other hesitant people will see that it can be done, and we're still alive."

Less than twenty miles from where John Anderson teaches high school, Dan Woog coaches soccer and teaches English at his alma mater, Staples High School in Westport, Connecticut. In addition to his work as an educator, Dan is also a writer. For over ten years, he has written a weekly column for the *Westport News*, "Woog's World," on topics of school and community interest.

In the early 1990s, Dan joined the National Gay and Lesbian Journalists Association and began writing for the gay press. "The more I did that," he says, "the more I realized that the time was coming when I had to be out publicly in Westport, and at Staples High School." In 1993, he attended the March on Washington (officially named the March for Lesbian, Gay, and Bisexual Equal Rights and Liberation), and returned feeling as if he "could have flown home without the plane." He immediately began working on a book about gay and lesbian issues in American schools, "from teachers' organizations to coming-out stories to athletics to school nurses and guidance counselors."

Telling people at school about the book was Dan's first step out of the closet, though he did not actually identify himself as gay. In the winter of 1994, the Staples librarian invited him to do a talk about his work-in-progress, as part of a series of presentations by local authors.

And here I was, local person. She put up these flyers: "Staples' own Dan Woog talks about gay and lesbian issues in America's schools." . . . Much to my delight and shock and worry, about three hundred and fifty people showed up. It was the largest [audience] they'd ever had. . . . Kids skipped class to come hear it.

Though Dan says he was prepared to come out if anybody asked, nobody did.

Right before the bell rang, a kid had his hand up in the back, a football player. . . . He said, "Yeah, I wanna know why schools have gay clubs [referring to the Gay/Straight Alliances that have been formed at many schools], why they don't have straight clubs." He sort of smirked while he said it, like he had pulled a fast one on me. And I felt as if he had tossed up this little softball that I could just blast out of the park.

Dan pointed out that "the world is really a straight club, and these gay and straight alliances are just ways that gays and straight kids can be allies to help educate the schools about homophobia." Just then, the bell rang. Down in the cafeteria, the same student told Dan he had "a really personal question to ask." But when Dan invited him to ask it, "he chickened out. He said, 'Oh, I'll ask you later.' And he never did."

Meanwhile, several girls approached Dan with the idea of starting a Gay/Straight Alliance at Staples. Another teacher, a heterosexual woman, immediately agreed to be the the cofacilitator. The group began meeting regularly, trying to think of ways that straight students could be allies for their gay classmates. During one of the final meetings of the 1993–94 school year, a girl expressed regret that despite the group's increasing visibility, no one in the school had come out that year.

I said, "Read the paper tomorrow." They all looked at me. I said, "My coming-out column appears tomorrow."

The piece in question was one that Dan had actually written several months earlier. "I was waiting for a really good time," he says. "And I just sort of felt that this was a good time." The response was phenomenal.

It's sort of a Staples tradition to have coffee on Friday mornings, coffee and donuts, and everybody sits around and deconstructs my columns. And this one, nobody said anything. . . . It was very quiet in the faculty room. And I walked into the cafeteria and there was an undercurrent. . . . It was clear that this news had swept the cafeteria while I was having coffee. Nobody knew how to react when I walked in. Then the captain of the soccer team walked up to me, stuck out his hand, and said, "Dan, great job. Congratulations, I'm really proud of you." And that sort of empowered or legitimized everyone—it let them realize that they could talk.

For the rest of the day, Dan says, he heard nothing but positive reactions from students.

I heard about all their gay and lesbian relatives. By the end of the day, I felt like, okay, we got a cousin over here on the left, we have an uncle on the right. And that relative I'll see right now.

Responses from teachers were equally positive, and occasionally surprising.

A guidance counselor came up as I was talking to a group of kids, and said, "So long as we're making confessions, I've had a crush on you for years. I always wondered what it would take to get you into bed." And as he walked away, the kids around me just stared. Yeah, adults talk about sex too.

In addition to all the positive face-to-face comments, Dan says, he received "a hundred and ten letters or notes, not one of which was negative." He also received fifty or sixty phone calls. "Everybody knows I have an answering machine. How hard would it be to leave an obscene or a nasty message on the machine? None. . . . It was wild."

A few days later, Dan was sitting with friends at the Westport Memorial Day Parade.

People would jump out of line . . . and shake my hand. . . . There were some people from New York, and they were just completely befuddled. "Who is this person? and why is he being congratulated?" And it struck me that it was strange being congratulated for such a thing, for basically just saying who you are. But at the same time I realized that it really tapped into strong feelings that people had.

A friend later told him, "Dan, that was wild. You came out to fifty thousand people at once." When Dan reminded the friend that the circulation of the *Westport News* was only ten thousand, his friend said, "Dan, everybody xeroxed that piece for five people."

Dan says that coming out "has taken an incredible weight off my shoulders, just in terms of the energy that I needed to pretend, to change pronouns." He knows that he has raised awareness at Staples and in the community to the point where many people have told him, "You have made me rethink everything I ever thought about gay people." But the most important reason to come out, he says, was his coaching.

I know both instinctively and from finding it out after the fact that I've coached many, many kids who were gay or questioning. And in the past, before I came out, not only was I not a positive role model for those kids, who could see that a gay man can accomplish a lot in the athletic world— but I was also not a positive role model for the straight kids because I allowed homophobic comments to continue. I would never let kids use racist or ethnic slurs, but if someone called another kid a faggot or something like that, I'd let it go.

Now, Dan says, homophobic remarks are no longer an issue because they rarely occur.

I know that most of the straight kids have never had any contact with some-body gay, especially somebody in the athletic world. And now here's a guy who's teaching us to be good soccer players and he's really hard on them on the field and being there for them off the field, and sharing the disappoint-ments and sharing the joys.

Being out to his students has brought Dan closer to his students, and allowed greater communication.

I find the kids are now much more willing to talk to me about anything. Personal problems. You know, their own fears and trepidations about life. There's no longer this wall up between us. Even though I was always pretty easy to talk to, and friendly, clearly now this wall is down.

Dan acknowledges that Westport, Connecticut, is "an elite environ-ment," home to many writers and artists. Though he knows his neighbors are no more intelligent than people elsewhere, he feels they have "a broader, deeper worldview. They come in contact with a lot of different people. They have resources." Yet even in the most privileged of environments, coming out as a teacher and coach is no small accomplishment. For Dan, it has provided the opportunity to show the students and staff at Staples High School that gay people are all around them. As he wrote in his coming-out column, published in the *Westport News* on May 27, 1994:

Straight people need to confront their own internalized homophobia; to put a familiar face on the words "gay" and "lesbian"; to talk, ask questions, discover how a number of other human beings live. They'll learn we're not a whole lot different from them.

16

Heroes of Their Own Stories

IN TERMS OF CULTURE AND GEOGRAPHY, WESTPORT, CON-
necticut, is light years away from Colorado Springs, Colorado, where Lyn
Boudreau teaches elementary school music. And it would be hard to find two
people who at first glance seem more different from one another than Dan,
the jock soccer coach and journalist, and Lyn, the earnest ex-nun who still
plays her guitar at folk masses and directs the local lesbian and gay choir. But
these two share more than just the fact that they are educators. Like Dan, Lyn
came out in a public and dramatic way, and like him, she was motivated by
the desire to be known as the person she really is.

Nevertheless, there is one significant difference between these two
teachers' stories. At about the time that Dan Woog was writing his column in
the relatively enlightened community of Westport, Connecticut, Lyn
Boudreau declared herself a lesbian in a state where the human and civil
rights of gay people—in fact, their very lives—were under attack.

Lyn began teaching public school in Colorado Springs in 1991, shortly
after leaving the Sisters of the Order of Saint Benedict, and just before the
beginning of the Amendment Two campaign. She had come out during her
years in the convent, when she found herself falling in love with another nun
and "coming to the truth of who I was." Not long after returning to lay life,
she started dating her partner, Betty Lynn. Because both of them were active
in the anti-Amendment Two movement, Lyn says, she felt "scared" as soon as
she started teaching public school.

> If I wasn't at a rally, I was at a political meeting. If I wasn't at a political
> meeting, I was planning a strategy to do handouts or leaflets, or going down

to the mall and talking about it. I was wearing my "No on Two" button. I was in the thick of it, in terms of this political battle against this horrible thing.

Lyn's motivation came from her desire "to be square with the world," a phrase she uses often.

I came out to as many people as I could at school. I found myself being more and more open about talking about the issue, and . . . about "this affects me." . . . I decided at that point that what I really wanted to do was talk about my relationship with Betty Lynn as others talked about their relationships with their spouses.

Even as she started coming out to her colleagues, Lyn struggled with the risks of identifying as a gay teacher in Colorado Springs in 1992.

There were rumors that they were witch-hunting teachers in District 11. But I had already talked to Betty Lynn about this during that whole time and we decided that if there was gonna be a test case, why not me? I was well loved at the school, well respected by the kids and the parents, and I knew I was good, and if they were gonna fault me, they were gonna have to really dig. . . . So I thought, well, who better? And was I willing to cross that line? And I discovered in my heart that I was willing to cross that line.

The day after Amendment Two was voted into law, Lyn joined the teachers union: "I wanted to be protected just in case someone wanted to bring a lawsuit against me." She also consulted her principal, who assured her that even though she was still a provisional teacher, Lyn was sure to be rehired in the fall. Lyn describes those days as a fearful time.

No one knew what was gonna happen. . . . The whole town—the lesbian and gay community especially—was kind of on edge. What does this really mean? What is it gonna change? How will it affect me at work? What are the legalities of me coming out now? What do I have to fear? Especially for teachers. . . . People were in shock. A lot of us didn't know what to do.

That spring, Colorado Springs' annual Gay Pride rally featured an event called "a walk across the stage." In the wake of the demoralizing defeat eight months earlier, members of the gay and lesbian community were invited up to the platform to celebrate themselves and their vocations.

Betty Lynn walked across as an electrician, and there were people who walked across as carpenters and everything. . . . I was the only school teacher who walked across the stage.

Lyn grows thoughtful as she tries to explain what motivated her to take that solitary walk.

> I wanted to see, well, what are we actually fearing here? What are you gonna do to me? Tell me I can't teach? You have to come against the union, then. I'm protected with my contract. Or just make it hard for me to teach by bringing up all kinds of lies against me? What are you gonna do? . . . So I walked across the stage.

Five minutes later, a reporter from the Colorado Springs *Gazette Telegraph* approached her for an interview. After thinking about it "for maybe two or three seconds," Lyn agreed to speak with him.

> I gave him some quotes about the day, about the fact that we were out here. Coloradans for Family Values [the group that had promoted the referendum] meant it for bad. Look at what's happened. It's been wonderful, strengthening. Look at the crowd here. It's strong, it's compassionate—you know, their worst fears have come true.

Lyn's quotation appeared in the next day's paper, complete with a preview box on the front page identifying her as "Lyn Boudreau, public school teacher." She was also featured in several local TV news segments. "And I used the pronoun 'us,' which self-identified me. . . . Here it was."

At four o'clock the next afternoon, Lyn received a call from her principal, informing her that her position as a music teacher had just been transformed into two part-time positions, and that two teachers had already been assigned to fill them. Lyn had been removed from her job.

> Well, of course, you know the wheels started turning. I was shocked. I had counted on it. [The principal] was shocked, 'cause she really wanted me back. . . . I went for the entire summer after that doing my own little search and detective work trying to see what this is really about. . . . And for the first time I thought, "Hmm, maybe this is how it hits."

Other gay teachers saw the turn of events as a vindication of their fears. "I had a lot of my friends who said, 'Now you know how it works, Lyn. You come out and it's no job, which is why we're scared.' . . . But I didn't want to believe that."

Lyn interviewed for three elementary positions, and in each case, was refused for reasons the administrators would not divulge: "Well, you just weren't a fit." Finally, someone who knew she needed a job was able to help her piece together a part-time assignment in a junior high and an elementary school.

Later that year, TV journalist Bill Moyers came to Colorado Springs to film a documentary on life after Amendment Two. When the crew of *Bill Moyers' Journal* heard about Lyn, the teacher who had walked across the stage, and Betty Lynn, her activist partner, they immediately wanted to include them in the story. Betty Lynn was interviewed about her work in the campaign; Lyn was shown playing her guitar at a church reception, and the two were filmed attending services at First Congregational Church, whose minister, Jim White, had announced their commitment ceremony before the entire congregation. The show appeared on November 19, 1993.

> The Monday after that aired, I got a little stack of handwritten harassment letters from a group of eighth-grade kids, pretty dirty stuff, awful stuff. . . . I read them through, about sixteen handwritten, pencilled-in things. I don't think it was that many kids who wrote the letters. I think it was maybe two or three that made it look like there was a lot of them, and just nasty stuff. . . . No real threats, but one said, "My mom says you shouldn't even be teaching and she's against you and she's never gonna talk to you again."

Lyn's colleagues were very supportive. "Two or three of 'em actually came up to me and said, 'Saw you on the show. Real good job. We're for you.'"

Teaching junior high school was not "a good fit" for Lyn, but she made the best of the situation. Shortly before school ended, she received a call from the district music supervisor. He had received "a stack of letters" from parents at her old school. "Everyone really wanted me back," she says. "I was really popular. It was wonderful." Through some judicious juggling, the district was able to put together a three-quarter time job at her former school, where she was glad to be back—"and open, and out." One year later, the principal offered her a regular full-time contract.

Lyn Boudreau is an openly gay teacher in the only state whose citizens have voted to deny basic civil rights to lesbians and gay men. In this atmosphere of fear and hatred, she has paid a price for her openness, and she knows that she may have to pay again in the future. But for Lyn, who sees the world in ethical terms, coming out means living her deepest beliefs. Though she may have left the convent, her words reveal that she still feels a moral obligation to whatever God has called her to do.

> I believe that the only way we're gonna get past the stuff that's happening and the fear is not in political activism, it's not in throwing rallies. I'm not

looking to the government to save me or a union to protect me. . . . We have to be out where we are as teachers. People need to see us as good, wholesome people who happen to be lesbian and gay, and let them deal with the dissonance.

Being out in school is Lyn's way of speaking the truth, not only about herself, but about all her sisters and brothers in the lesbian and gay community.

I need to be an example for this town that teachers can live a good life and be lesbian and gay and be out, that I'm a good person. People need to know that we're wonderful people. . . . And let CFV [Coloradans for Family Values] and Focus on the Family see me. . . . If they're gonna pick on someone, then look at my record. Look at who I am with kids.

Colorado was one of the first two states where proponents of so-called family values placed referendum questions on the ballot. The most recent addition to the list is Maine. But even before Question One reached the voters of Maine, gay rights bills had been debated in the legislature for over fifteen years. For most of those years, the bill was defeated; in 1993, it passed both houses but was vetoed by Republican Governor John McKernan. Each year, more and more lesbians and gay men have come forward to testify about their own experiences of discrimination in housing, employment, finance, and public accommodations. In 1989, a new voice was added to the public debate—that of Alan Kelly-Hamm, the first teacher in Maine to testify publicly as a gay man.

Alan had already been a VISTA volunteer, a day-care worker, and an English language teacher in Japan when he was hired as a substitute teacher and part-time sign language interpreter in an elementary school in rural Waldo County. Since his position at the school was a temporary one, Alan had already made plans to enter graduate school and pursue his regular teaching certificate, when the *Waldo Independent* called around the third week of May. A reporter was looking for a gay man to comment on discrimination in Maine. Would Alan consent to be interviewed?

At that point, Maine's lesbian and gay civil rights bill had just been defeated "for the umpteenth time." Both legislators from Alan's district had voted against the bill because they were sure that there was no discrimination in Waldo County. State Representative Francis Marsano, a first-generation Italian American, made a point of telling the *Independent* that he "knew discrimination when he saw it," and would never allow it in Waldo County. But no gay man or lesbian had ever approached him with a complaint. Alan volunteered to talk to the reporter.

> I gave my name. I didn't want a picture; I thought, that's one step too far. But I said, "Look, the discrimination is here." I talked about an incident where a first-grade teacher would not allow a little boy to sit on my lap— for whatever reason, it was never stated. I talked about the subtle discrimination of never being able to name your life . . . and how you can get fired in this state for being gay. You're not even entitled to fair hearings in a lot of places. I named it.

The publication of the interview "royally pissed off" the two state legislators, according to Alan, "but I said what I needed to say." Then he prepared to return to his classroom.

> I told my allies, "I did this interview, and I need you there for me. I'm scared shitless." They got the paper that day, they called me up, they said, "This is a great interview." I said, "Hold my hand tomorrow, because I am going to need it." I went to school and nobody said a word. Good old Maine tradition—nobody said a word.

Perhaps, as Alan suggests, the silence was due to Yankee reticence, or perhaps it came from his situation as a temporary teacher about to leave for graduate school. Whatever the reason, the few comments he did receive were completely favorable.

> Melissa was in the first grade. Her mother came up to me and said, "I'm going to save this interview, and when Melissa is old enough to read it, I want her to read it." Every time I see her shopping she says, "I want you to come by and have coffee. Melissa would love to see you." I feel like that has validated the whole thing.

Nevertheless, Alan is a realist about social change. He believes that homophobia is "a cultural issue. . . . We are the last open targets." He calls Maine "probably a better place than many rural states, but you've got a lot of narrow minds in any situation, not just rural situations." But Alan is proud of having coming out, and proud of being a good teacher.

> I don't feel like spending all my life trying to educate people on issues. Which is why I go back to kids. Because there is hope for kids. . . . If I reach a handful of kids in any one class and they take any of what I've given them out into the world, I've accomplished something.

Dan Dromm is a political activist who has battled conservative politicians and reactionary newspaper columnists. But his coming out in the New York City school system was prompted by the tears of a nine-year-old girl in Dan's fourth-grade class at P.S. 199, Sunnyside, Queens.

Dan has been a teacher for nearly twenty years, eleven of them at P.S. 199. His school is located in a mostly Hispanic, poor, and working-class area of District Twenty-four, which in 1992 seemed like the last place in the world that a gay teacher would want to come out.

The controversy dated back to 1989, when the New York City Board of Education passed a resolution calling for a new multicultural curriculum to promote diversity in the New York City public schools. The following summer, a gay Latino man named Julio Rivera was murdered by two skinheads who later told police that they had been looking for a gay victim. The affair sparked the outrage of both the gay and the Latino communities, and led to the inclusion of lesbian and gay families in the new curriculum, "Children of the Rainbow." Five school districts in Brooklyn, the Bronx, and Staten Island voted to reject the sections of the curriculum dealing with lesbians and gays; District Twenty-four rejected the entire curriculum.

Meanwhile, on a spring afternoon, one of Dan Dromm's fourth graders came in after lunch, crying bitterly.

> I said to her, "What's wrong, honey? What's the matter? Why are you crying?" And she just let out a burst and she said, "They're teasing me because my mother's a lesbian." . . . And the only thing I could say to her at that point was, "Well, so long as you have a loving family, then you have a good family."

All summer, Dan was haunted by the memory of the little girl he had not come out to. He remembers thinking, "What could I have done differently? Or what would I like to be able to do differently in the future?"

At the end of the summer, school-board president Mary Cummins—a leader in the fight against the Children of the Rainbow curriculum—sent a letter to the district's forty-four thousand parents calling for a massive protest outside the New York City Board of Education offices. "We will not accept two people of the same sex engaged in deviant sex practices as 'family,'" the letter declared, and went on to attack the AIDS/HIV curriculum that had been endorsed by Chancellor Joseph Fernandez: "The victims of this AIDS scourge are homosexuals, bisexuals, intravenous users of illicit drugs, and the innocent people they infect by exposing them to their tainted blood and other body fluids."

For Dan Dromm, this was the final straw. "We had our own Colorado in our own backyard, in New York City," he says. "One of the most liberal cities in the world winds up having a school district full of bigots."

Dan's moment of truth came at a meeting of the Lesbian and Gay Community Services Center in Manhattan, which had been called to develop a response to events in District Twenty-four.

> I went to the meeting with a friend of mine. I knew the whole time I was driving there that if I raised my hand and said I was a teacher in District Twenty-four, then a lot of shit was gonna hit the fan, so to speak. But I decided to do it.

Two days later, Dan was interviewed by a reporter from *New York Newsday*, the New York/Long Island daily.

> I had never really come out to my principal . . . so once I did the interview I felt I had to give my principal the courtesy of telling him. I said to him, "There's gonna be a tiny article and a picture in tomorrow's paper on my support for the Children of the Rainbow curriculum." "Well," he says, "I trust you and that what you've done is what you feel is right."

On Friday, September 25, an article headlined "Gay Teachers Speak Out" appeared in *Newsday*, with a banner headline and a big picture of Dan at school ("I never saw a picture so large in a newspaper in my life," he says). Things happened so fast that Dan did not even have time to warn his mother about his impending fame; she first saw the article and picture when she picked up a copy of *Newsday* to search the classifieds for an apartment. Luckily, Dan was already out to her, though he says wryly, "I remember that her reaction was, 'now I'm gonna have to tell all the relatives.'"

That afternoon, Sandra Feldman, President of the United Federation of Teachers, called a press conference which included statements by Dan and Kim Kriecker, a lesbian teacher who had also come out in the *Newsday* article.

> It was everything that you think a news conference would be, with like a hundred reporters, all the camera lights, and in comes Sandra Feldman, very authoritative, president of this huge union. . . . We went in and she said, "Let me start off by saying that nothing—repeat, nothing—is going to happen to these teachers. . . . These are both excellent teachers. That's our position. Nobody will take any actions against either of these teachers."

The press conference was featured on the front page of the *New York Times* Metro section the following day, as well as in dozens of other newspapers and radio and TV reports. Editorials in both the *Times* and *Newsday* defended the Children of the Rainbow curriculum; the *Newsday* editorial said that Dan and Kim had "put a human face on the issue of discrimination." Encouraged, Dan resolved to "take those fifteen minutes of fame and turn it into something more permanent." He decided that "the best response to Mary Cummins would be to show people that we live here in Queens . . . so I pulled together a committee, which we named the Queens Lesbian and Gay Pride Committee." The committee organized Queens' first Lesbian and Gay Pride Parade in June 1993.

> Ten thousand people showed up. So we kind of now jokingly say that Mary Cummins was the mother of the parade, and we even jokingly thought about making her the honorary Grand Marshall.

One person who was not amused by the growing visibility of Queens' lesbian and gay community was Howard Hurwitz, a former public school principal and voraciously homophobic columnist for the local *Ridgewood Times Weekly*. In a column written not long after the first Queens parade, Hurwitz cast suspicion on the gubernatorial campaign of Manhattan Borough President Ruth Messinger because of Messinger's open support for her lesbian daughter, Miriam. In a letter to the editor that was as alliterative as it was determined, Dan suggested that "horrible Howard Hurwitz' homophobic harangue helps homosexuals," inspiring them to come out and refute the lies about themselves. He concluded the letter, "I came out to my fourth-grade class in response to Howard and his cohort, Mary Cummins," and signed it, "Daniel P. Dromm, teacher."

What happened next could have been predicted, given the political climate in District Twenty-four. When school opened in the fall, Dan was called into the principal's office for a disciplinary hearing to discuss the letter, particularly the part that said, "I came out to my fourth-grade class." Dan objected.

> I told him I didn't think that they had any right to bring me in, that there was a New York City law that protected us from discrimination. . . . My response was that when I was presented with articles or questions by the children . . . I always admitted that I was gay.

Though the principal reiterated his respect for Dan as an excellent teacher, the school board wrote up the incident as a case of unprofessional behavior. Dan is appealing the matter to the New York City Human Rights Commission, where after a failed attempt at mediation, it awaits further investigation.

Meanwhile Dan's most enthusiastic supporters are the children in his fourth-grade class. One little girl drew a picture of two figures, one labeled "Mr. Dromm," and the other labeled "Me." "Mr. Dromm" is saying, "I am happy I'm gay," as the little girl in the picture responds, "Say it louder, Mr. Dromm, I like that everybody would know and mine there buisness[*sic*]."

Like other gay teachers who have taken the risk of full disclosure, Dan Dromm says that coming out of the closet "has been the most positive thing that I ever could have done. . . . I had been out for twenty years, and I never fully realized what it meant to come out." And like other out teachers, he knows his struggle is part of a wider movement.

> We've gotten so far, but the classic opposition to the lesbian and gay movement is that in some way we are unfit to be around children. I think that the more we knock down that wall, the [better] off we're gonna be as a community.

Dan acknowledges that not all gay teachers can expect the kind of support he enjoys: "I imagine that if we didn't have the gay civil rights bill [in New York City], I probably wouldn't be working now." Yet he believes that gay teachers must take risks in any way they can, because "education, and specifically lesbian and gay teachers and dealing with lesbian and gay youth, is the fight that the lesbian and gay movement needs to battle for the next twenty years."

Bayport, New York, is a small suburban town on Long Island's south shore. Its residents "voted for Reagan and voted for Bush and are anti-Clinton . . . a rather conservative group of people," according to Bob Bradley, who has taught in the Bayport school district for twenty-five years. Yet in the summer of 1990, the people of Bayport rallied behind a junior high school teacher who had come out to them as a gay man with AIDS. That man was Bob Bradley's twin brother Tom, and the story of Bayport and the Bradley brothers is a story of love and support in some unlikely places.

As young men, Bob and Tom followed similar paths. Both entered the seminary intending to become Catholic priests; both left to become teachers after realizing they were gay. Bob came out of the closet before his brother, and the resulting conflict precipitated a split that lasted for two years. During that time, they barely spoke to each other, though they were teaching in the same district.

Eventually, the Bradley brothers were reconciled and moved into an apartment in Queens. For twenty years, they lived the divided life so familiar to gay teachers, cultivating a circle of gay friends in New York and remaining mostly closeted at school. During that time, they earned the love and respect of countless Bayport parents and children. They took dozens of fifth-grade classes on an annual trip to Washington, and Tom designed and planned an extensive computer lab that now bears his name. He was president of the union and district teacher of the year. "You do for your kids what's best for your kids," says Bob. "When you earn the respect of people, then you get it."

In 1990, the respect of the people of Bayport received the ultimate test. Tom Bradley told his community that he had AIDS. Although he had managed to keep his HIV-positive status a secret for seven years, Tom could no longer hide his illness when he began losing weight. "He told people at first that he had colitis. And then he told people that he had Crohn's disease. And then, cancer."

That summer, Tom and Bob's family doctor learned of an experimental AIDS treatment at Johns Hopkins Medical Center. Because Tom and Bob were identical twins, researchers theorized that Tom's body would not reject Bob's bone marrow, which might build new tissue free of HIV. The brothers traveled to Baltimore, where they were approved for the procedure. But when their insurance company, which had initially agreed to pay for the treatment, suddenly backed down, the brothers were faced with a momentous decision. Attorneys at Lambda Legal Defense and Education fund, a national lesbian and gay advocacy organization, advised them that their only hope was to put pressure on the insurance company by going public.

> We sat down, the two of us, and he said to me that legally in the state of New York, if you have HIV you cannot be discriminated against. You have the protection of the law. He said to me, "They can't fire me. They can find a pretense to fire you, so you have to make the decision." And my response to him was, "We're fighting for your life. There's no issue here. We have to go public with it. If I lose my job, I lose my job."

Bob admits that at the time he did think he might lose his job. "This is a conservative, Republican school district. And Long Island is typical middle class." But when a small article appeared in *Newsday*, announcing that "a gay teacher had sued his insurance company," the community's response was beyond anything Tom or Bob could have anticipated.

> It was a Saturday evening. The two of us sat here . . . with my lover and Tom's best friend, when the phone rang. . . . And it was a teacher to tell me

that the kids were out in the community going door-to-door and asking people to sign a petition urging the insurance company to pay for his transplant.

The response by Bayport's children was only the beginning. Students, former students, and members of the community wrote letters to the editor supporting their teacher. Parents organized Tom Bradley Day, a fund-raising festival to help defray the brothers' travel costs to Baltimore. In all the outpouring of support, there was only one negative letter to the editor of the local newspaper, and it was immediately followed by indignant responses from several former students.

A few months later, the insurance company capitulated. But it was too late. When Tom and Bob arrived at Hopkins, doctors discovered that Tom had already developed an opportunistic infection, making him ineligible for the bone marrow transplant. Bob Bradley holds the insurance company responsible.

> The infection was only about two or three weeks old, if that. . . . Although to be quite frank, I think he would have never survived the process. There were three other people who had the transplant, and I don't think any of them survived. [Hopkins has since discontinued the procedure.]

Though the operation might not have saved Tom's life, Bob believes that it might have given him more time and allowed him the opportunity to "die fighting."

When Tom and Bob returned home, everyone knew what had happened in Baltimore. But, Tom Bradley Day, which had already been scheduled for the beginning of the 1990 school year, went on as planned.

> Literally, there were thousands of people. It was like a big fair, and festival. And he was very deeply moved by it because, as he said, it is very rare that someone gets the opportunity to hear the wonderful things that people say about them, because usually you're dead when these tributes come. . . . People were saying to him, "Thank you for what you've done for our kids. You have been there always for them. Now we're being there for you."

Because Tom was so well known and loved in the community, Bob says, "it wasn't the gay issue or the straight issue, it was people who were responding to a human being who they respect and who they were saying thank you to. It didn't make a difference that he was gay. And that's the way it should be."

Tom Bradley finished the school year, and was even able to take his mother on a long-anticipated trip to Europe that summer. Finally, he was brought to the hospital, where he spent his last day with Bob at his side, "correcting papers, reading papers to him, and asking his opinion."

Several months after Tom's death, his brother was approached by Glenn Jordan, an Emmy-winning television producer and director. Jordan had read Tom's obituary in the *New York Times*, and wanted to make a movie about the story.

> We sat at lunch for about four hours. At the end of it he said, "I want to do this story, and you have my commitment." . . . My fear was that they were going to sensationalize and destroy the story and twist it around. I didn't want a fag story, I didn't want a homosexual story, I wanted a story told about my brother. And he turned around and said to me, "I don't do those kinds of stories."

Bob finally agreed to the project, for several reasons. "One, to say thank you to my community. And two, to show the world how special they are." In addition, he hoped the movie would help others accept gay family members and family members with HIV. His own mother had "a very hard time" accepting her sons' homosexuality, but has "moved a whole 180 degrees" toward acceptance of Bob and his partner as members of the family.

On March 19, 1995, *My Brother's Keeper* aired nationally on CBS-TV, starring John Lithgow in a dual role as Tom and Bob Bradley. Bob was delighted with the film.

> I thought it was sensitive. I thought it treated his homosexuality—our homosexuality—in its proper perspective. It wasn't the center of our lives, it's part of our lives.

The students and parents of Bayport reacted to seeing themselves and their gay teachers in a TV movie much as they had reacted to the Bradley brothers' press conference in the summer of 1990.

> Kids came in with pictures, they came in with clippings from the advertisement and the promos and the *TV Guide* and the newspaper articles from *Newsday*. Not one of them asked me about being gay. Now, I teach middle school—and you know, seventh and eighth graders can be extraordinarily hard and cruel when they want to be. Not a word.

During the lawsuit, and especially after the showing of *My Brother's Keeper*, Bob Bradley became something of a celebrity in Bayport. But when he talks about his life as an out gay teacher, he sounds like any other newly out educator, reveling in the freedom of not having to hide.

Everyone assumes that I'm gay because they now know. That's perhaps one of the most wonderful things about coming out of the closet and being accepted. Now a phone call comes in and if it's my lover, they hunt me down and say, "Bob, Luis is on the line." Whereas in the past they wouldn't pass his phone calls through. "Well, he's in class right now." And they would leave a message, "Your friend Luis called." They accept our relationship as they know who he is and how important he is to me. And that's wonderful. That's very liberating.

Bob Bradley has told his story to countless newspaper and TV reporters. Each time, interviewers ask the same question: "Why?" Why did two gay teachers, one of whom was living with AIDS, receive so much support from a White, middle-class community on Long Island? Part of the answer, Bob responds, lies in the fact that the Bradley brothers were a known quantity, two devoted teachers who had been loved and admired for twenty years. Bob is also quick to point out that though they may be traditional, the citizens of Bayport are far from reactionary; the district has implemented a progressive AIDS curriculum that begins in the primary grades. At times, Bob admits, the town's reaction is something of a mystery even to him: "I don't know why they are so different than everyone else." But when pressed to offer an explanation, he returns to one of the key moments in the film.

They attributed the quote to the superintendent of schools, but actually it was the president of the teachers union who said it. When the press asked, "Why? Why? Why so different for this human being?"—his response, I thought, was very, very wise. "The forces of good acted before the forces of evil could react." People don't like to oppose a bandwagon. And I think that's what happened here. There was an immediate positive reaction. So that if there were people out there who were negative, they kept it rather silent.

In a *New York Times* article about *My Brother's Keeper*, producer Glenn Jordan was quoted as saying that the community of Bayport "is the real hero in this story." Bob Bradley, who is extremely modest about his teaching accomplishments, would probably agree. But Bob and Tom are also the heroes of their own story. Like other gay teachers who have refused to live a lie, they changed their lives and the lives of their students and community through the simple courage to be themselves.

Few gay teachers step out of the closet in front of newspaper reporters and television cameras. Most live relatively anonymous lives, where their daily risks and triumphs are known only to a small circle of colleagues and friends. But like Bob Bradley, they are all struggling to live authentic lives in their classrooms and schools. Every photo on the desk, every refusal to use the "Monday-morning pronoun," every challenge to the slur overheard in the hallway, is a way of saying, "I am here. I am lesbian or gay. I am a teacher. I am a whole person." Now it is up to us, the parents, teachers, administrators, and students who consider ourselves allies, to match this courage. For the sake of our teachers, our schools and our children, we can do no less.

Epilogue

I learned that I am still on the journey, even though I have been discouraged. So I remind myself that I can do this.

—High school teacher

IT'S LATE FRIDAY AFTERNOON WHEN THE TEACHERS START arriving. Suitcases and duffel bags in tow, they pause in the doorway to look around, as if to reassure themselves that it's safe to proceed. After a moment, they catch sight of the table in the middle of the room with the sign that says "Registration" and the smiling young woman sitting behind it. Reassured, but still a bit hesitant, they approach one at a time to give their names.

For the next two and a half days, these men and women will laugh together, cry together, eat and work together. They will share their personal stories and their classroom experiences, their struggles and their triumphs. But they will share something more, something many of them have never shared with anyone in the profession. All of the teachers in this group are lesbian, gay, or bisexual, and they have come to take part in a unique experience: Project Empowerment.

Project Empowerment was born nine years ago, when a small group of teachers approached Carole Johnson, Deputy Director of the Equity Institute, with the idea of getting together to talk about the issues they shared as lesbian and gay educators. As a lesbian and a former teacher, Carole immediately recognized the importance of a retreat for gay educators. "I taught junior high school special education in Danbury and New Haven [Connecticut] for five and a half years," she says. "There's no way I could have been out."

The first PE retreat took place at Wolman Hill, a Quaker conference center in the hills of western Massachusetts. Since then, Project Empowerment has trained teachers in New York City, Chicago, Minneapolis–St. Paul, northern and southern California, and Washington State. In 1994, Equity decided to concentrate on places where referendum initiatives have placed lesbian and gays under political attack, and has brought PE to Oregon; Colorado; Dade County, Florida; and Portland, Maine.

The teachers, librarians, social workers, administrators, and counselors who gather on this warm spring afternoon have come from many places. Some teach in urban centers where they are implicitly or explicitly out; others work in rural communities where hostility toward lesbians and gays is overt and frightening. One man, a school media specialist, has driven over six hours from his home in a rural part of the state, where the local ministers publicly denounced the opening of a lesbian and gay community center.

The first hours are spent settling in; roommates are assigned, gear is unpacked, and everyone assembles for dinner in an atmosphere of anticipation. The conversation is about teaching and teachers—students, curriculum, classroom anecdotes—not very different from what one might overhear at any gathering of educators near the end of a school year. Afterward, we assemble in the large, comfortable meeting room where we will be spending most of our time for the next two days.

The focus of this first evening is getting to know each other. The workshop leaders introduce themselves: besides Carole, there is Jonathan Poullard, a young African American gay man from Los Angeles who has worked with Project Empowerment for the past three years, and Megan Smith, an Equity apprentice trainer. I am introduced as a straight ally and observer writing a book about lesbian and gay teachers. I wonder how the participants will feel about having an outsider present, but when Carole mentions that I am past president of my local P-FLAG chapter, everyone smiles, and I am no longer an outsider.

The rest of the evening is devoted to getting acquainted. Everyone tells their coming-out stories—tales of adolescent crushes on teachers and coaches, of parents who tried to haul them off to therapists and parents who said they had known all along, straight friends who became hostile or who reached out as allies, ex-spouses and children who reacted with rejection or unexpected support. They are the stories that enliven any gathering of lesbians and gay men, and the people in this group have told them before. But tonight is different. No one here has ever shared a coming-out story with a roomful of other educators. There are nods of profound understanding, and hugs of encouragement. There is much laughter, and tears. At the end of the evening, one of the men in the group says, "I can't believe how close I feel to the people in this group."

Saturday morning is devoted to a discussion of oppression and exclusion, with a good dose of theory. Carole and Jonathan talk about "targets" and "agents"—designations indicating the power relationship between two groups of people. The goal is for people in "target" groups (gay, lesbian, and bisexual people, people of color, disabled people) to become "empowered," and for those in "agent" groups (straight people, White people, able-bodied people) to become "allies," or advocates for those with less power. Within this framework, lesbian and gay teachers can be allies for people in other groups even as they seek to empower themselves.

For some people, this analysis is a welcome new way of putting their own experiences into a wider context. Others are beginning to look restless, and during the break that follows, I hear some grumbling, some wondering when we're going to get down to talking about schools. But the second part of the morning is directly related to people's lives as teachers. Group members brainstorm a list of qualities they value in allies, and post it on newsprint: the qualities include "understanding," "sensitivity," "respect," "humor." Good allies, according to the list, "do the right thing because it is the right thing to do." They "ask me what *I* want," and they are "appalled, amazed, offended by injustice." As the list develops, I find myself pondering the implications of all this for me, a heterosexual observer trying to tell the stories of lesbian and gay educators, and wondering how I measure up as an ally. At this moment, I am learning to listen without talking—a skill that does not come easily to a teacher educator who has led many workshops and told many people how to solve their problems.

We break for lunch. Afterward, the group talks about identity. "Caucuses" who share a particular identity—women, people of color, people with mental or physical disabilities—are asked to meet briefly and return to the group to tell their stories and enlighten others about how they can become allies. Afterward, members of the big group are asked to respond to the stories with comments that begin, "I heard . . ." The strongest reaction comes from the White members of the group after the presentation by the people of color: "I heard a lot of anger." Perhaps racism is still the hardest issue for White people to confront. Yet as they talk, and as they listen, everyone is beginning to realize that becoming an ally for others is an integral part of empowering oneself.

The afternoon break is a time for short walks and quiet reflection. Some people are writing in journals; others continue the conversations that began during the last part of the workshop. When we resume, there is a growing energy in the room that contrasts markedly with the restrained mood of our first dinner on Friday. The group has been together for less than twenty-four hours, yet I can already see alliances forming, lives changing.

The rest of the afternoon is devoted to a discussion about coming out in school. Carole and Jonathan present Pat Griffin's schematized version of coming out ("hiding," "covering," "implicitly out," "explicitly out"), and the teachers are invited to place themselves somewhere on the continuum. Carole invites all those who have actually come out in their schools to stand; about eight or nine people identify themselves. Then, she asks those who are no longer experiencing targeting to sit down. Only two people do so. Those who remain standing are a necessary object lesson: coming out in school may be empowering, but it does not necessarily make a teacher more safe. At the same time, Carole tells us that about 60 percent of the almost one thousand teachers who have been trained at Project Empowerment workshops have come out in their schools, and to the best of her knowledge, not one of these teachers has been fired.

Saturday night's program is a talent show, organized and presented by members of the group. When Carole announced this event on Friday, there were groans; yet in the end, everybody performs to enthusiastic applause. There is a silly song about geography and a lively puppet show. There are recitations and dances. Teachers congratulate one another on just how talented they all are. It is a time to rest from the hard work of the past day and a half and have fun together.

Sunday morning. Time for problem solving. The first step is another brainstorming exercise, again involving ally building. Teachers are asked to talk about the heterosexual allies they have already identified. What makes those people safe? How might they find others? One middle school teacher says, "I'm always putting feelers out, and I wait to see if anybody bites." A school counselor chimes in, "I really need to be out to my principal." An elementary teacher, the youngest person in the group, declares, "I need to connect with several straight men in my school. I need to make *sure* that they know I'm gay. I need to introduce them to my spouse."

Carole talks about the risks of reaching out to allies and the pain of disappointment when they don't meet expectations. "We give up on people too easily when we've been hurt," she says. "We expect perfection from allies. We should assume that our allies will make mistakes, and prepare to be disappointed. But we need to continue to expect the best from them."

Now the group divides into four subgroups, K–5, Middle School, Senior High, and Community. Each is assigned to come up with a list of problems, and then to select one outstanding problem and devise a strategic plan of action. Since I am still an observer, I wander around the room, eavesdropping. The scene is familiar—small, earnest groups of teachers with markers and newsprint, engrossed in strategizing and planning. But the phrases I hear when I listen closely are not those I have heard at an inservice or staff-development workshop—phrases like "homophobia," and "sexual minority families," and "Gay/Straight Alliance."

When we reconvene, the groups report back and Carole collects a master list of problems and strategies, which she will later assemble and mail to everybody. The elementary and middle groups want to design curricula with positive images of lesbian, gay, and bisexual people, and to address teasing and name-calling. They will work for staff training directed at targeting, and will begin teaching children how to be allies. The senior high group says that their most significant problem is an unsafe school environment. They propose greater visibility for lesbian and gay issues through diversity days, bulletin board displays, and more vigilant attention to harassment in classrooms and halls. Within the community group, whose members are mostly from small towns and rural areas, there is consensus that the most significant problem is invisibility and "denial," both inside and outside the gay community. "Too many causes and not enough people," they say. Their strategies focus on supporting lesbians and gay men who come out, and becoming more visible themselves. "Come out to someone you trust," says one group member, and another adds, "Come out to someone you don't know you can trust."

Finally, everyone develops a list of "next steps." The group agrees to continue meeting regularly. One man has access to electronic mail and a computerized data base; he will be responsible for keeping the mailing list and sending out notices. A teacher at an independent school is planning to start a Gay/Straight Alliance; she will let everyone know about her progress and encourage others to start similar groups at their schools. The social workers and counselors want to set up a "think tank" for lesbians and gays in school support services. Each person writes a personal contract, committing himself or herself to at least one personal "next step," whether it is coming out to another teacher at school, introducing a gay-themed novel into a reading curriculum, or becoming visible as an ally for lesbian and gay youth. Each contract is witnessed and signed by another member of the group, and each pair commits to checking in with one another regularly.

Unbelievably, it is time for farewells. Everyone is encouraged to offer appreciations for one another, and to share what they have learned about themselves. Their words show as clearly as anything why this workshop is called Project Empowerment.

I learned that I am really ready to make some important steps.

I have learned that I have something valuable to offer this group as a teacher and as a lesbian.

I learned that I am still on the journey, even though it has been sidetracked and I have been stuck and discouraged. I challenged myself to come here. I stuck with it and tried to be open to everything around me. So I remind myself that I can do this—whatever this is.

Finally, I am invited to join the circle with my own response to the weekend. I look at these teachers who have begun to transform their lives, and I think of all the other gay and lesbian teachers who have shared their stories with me. All of their struggles, all of their fears, are transformed within this circle of love and pride. I tell the group what is in my heart: hearing their stories teaches me what we all can be—what we already are.